CPCU 520 Course Guide

Insurance Operations
1st Edition

The Institutes
720 Providence Road, Suite 100
Malvern, Pennsylvania 19355-3433

1st Edition • 1st Printing • October 2010

ISBN 978-0-89463-431-4

Contents

 ## Study Materials Available for CPCU 520

Insurance Operations, 1st ed., 2010, AICPCU.

CPCU 520 *Course Guide*, 1st ed., AICPCU (includes access code for SMART Online Practice Exams).

CPCU 520 SMART Study Aids—Review Notes and Flash Cards, 1st ed.

Student Resources

Catalog A complete listing of our offerings can be found in *Succeed,* The Institutes' professional development catalog, including information about:

- Current programs and courses
- Current textbooks, course guides, SMART Study Aids, and online offerings
- Program completion requirements
- Exam registration

To obtain a copy of the catalog, visit our Web site at www.TheInstitutes.org or contact Customer Service at (800) 644-2101.

How to Prepare for Institutes Exams This free handbook is designed to help you by:

- Giving you ideas on how to use textbooks and course guides as effective learning tools
- Providing steps for answering exam questions effectively
- Recommending exam-day strategies

The handbook is printable from the Student Services Center on The Institutes' Web site at www.TheInstitutes.org, or available by calling Customer Service at (800) 644-2101.

Educational Counseling Services To ensure that you take courses matching both your needs and your skills, you can obtain free counseling from The Institutes by:

- E-mailing your questions to advising@TheInstitutes.org
- Calling an Institutes' counselor directly at (610) 644-2100, ext. 7601
- Obtaining and completing a self-inventory form, available on our Web site at www.TheInstitutes.org or by contacting Customer Service at (800) 644-2101

Exam Registration Information As you proceed with your studies, be sure to arrange for your exam.

- Visit our Web site at www.TheInstitutes.org/forms to access and print the Registration Booklet, which contains information and forms needed to register for your exam.
- Plan to register with The Institutes well in advance of your exam.

How to Contact The Institutes For more information on any of these publications and services:

- Visit our Web site at www.TheInstitutes.org
- Call us at (800) 644-2101 or (610) 644-2100 outside the U.S.
- E-mail us at customerservice@TheInstitutes.org
- Fax us at (610) 640-9576
- Write to us at The Institutes, Customer Service, 720 Providence Road, Suite 100, Malvern, PA 19355-3433

Using This Course Guide

This course guide will help you learn the course content and prepare for the exam.

Each assignment in this course guide typically includes the following components:

Educational Objectives These are the most important study tools in the course guide. Because all of the questions on the exam are based on the Educational Objectives, the best way to study for the exam is to focus on these objectives.

For each assignment, you should define or describe each of the Key Words and Phrases and answer each of the Review and Application Questions.

Educational Objective 1
Explain how insurers have organized to provide property-casualty insurance.

Key Words and Phrases

Proprietary insurer

Mutual insurer

Reciprocal insurance exchange (interinsurance exchange)

Fair Access to Insurance Requirements (FAIR) plans

Residual market

Surplus lines broker

Independent agency and brokerage marketing system

Direct writer marketing system

Exclusive agency marketing system

Distribution channel

Review Questions

1-1.   Identify the four classifications that may be used to distinguish property-casualty insurers from one another.

1-2.   How do stock and mutual insurers differ?

1-3.   Describe the role of each of these types of insurers.

   a.   Lloyd's of London

b. Reciprocal insurance exchanges

1-4. What is a domestic insurer?

1-5. What does it mean when an insurer is licensed in a state?

1-6. List some common distribution channels that insurers use to promote products and services and to communicate with existing and prospective insureds.

Educational Objective 2
Describe the major goals of an insurer.

Review Questions

2-1. Explain how insurers earn money to meet their profit goal.

2-2. Explain why the goal of meeting customers' needs can often conflict with the profit goal.

2-3. Explain how compliance with legal requirements helps an insurer meet its goals.

2-4. Explain why diversifying risk has become an emerging goal for property-casualty insurers.

2-5. Describe several ways that insurers fulfill their duty to society.

Educational Objective 3
Describe the internal and external constraints that impede insurers from achieving their major goals.

Key Word or Phrase
Probable maximum loss (PML)

Review Questions

3-1. Explain how an insurer's inefficiency in information technology can conflict with the insurer's customer needs and profit goals.

3-2. What advantages (representing fewer constraints) do larger insurers have over small insurers in meeting their goals?

3-3. In addition to efficiency, expertise, size, and financial resources, identify and explain two examples of other internal constraints that interfere with insurers' achieving their goals.

3-4. Explain how the external constraint of required regulatory approvals prevents insurers from meeting their profit and customer needs goals.

3-5. Explain how public opinion about the insurance industry as a whole acted as a constraint for some insurers in meeting their goals following catastrophic hurricane damages in the 2000s.

3-6. Explain how competition during a soft underwriting cycle becomes an external constraint for insurers in meeting their goals.

3-7. Explain how the increase in insurers' experimenting with multiple distribution systems and channels becomes an external constraint for insurers in meeting their goals.

Educational Objective 4
Describe the measurements used to evaluate how successful an insurer is at meeting its established goals.

Review Questions

4-1. What are two indicators of insurer profitability based on premiums?

4-2. What are the indicators that insurers can use to gauge their success in meeting customers' needs?

4-3. An insurer's success or failure in meeting legal requirements is indicated by the number of criminal, civil, and regulatory actions taken against the insurer. Three sources for measuring the success of the insurer include these:

4-4. Explain how expenditures on loss control activities indicate an insurer's level of humanitarian concern and can be a measure of how well an insurer meets social responsibilities.

Educational Objective 5
Describe the core and supporting functions performed by insurers.

Key Words and Phrases

Underwriting

Book of business

Underwriting guidelines (underwriting guide)

Adverse selection

Review Questions

5-1. Identify three core functions that exist within the structure of a typical insurer.

5-2. Identify five supporting functions that exist within the structure of a typical insurer.

5-3. Identify six other common functional areas that may exist within the structure of an insurer or that may be outsourced to an external organization.

Answers to Assignment 1 Questions

NOTE: These answers are provided to give students a basic understanding of acceptable types of responses. They often are not the only valid answers and are not intended to provide an exhaustive response to the questions.

Educational Objective 1

1-1. The four classifications that may be used to distinguish property-casualty insurers from one another are these:

- Legal form of ownership

- Place of incorporation

- Licensing status

- Insurance distribution systems and channels

1-2. A stock insurer is owned by its stockholders, who elect a board of directors to oversee the operations. Dividends from investments in stock insurers are returned to the shareholders. Mutual companies are owned by policyholders, who elect a board of directors. Profits in excess of those added to surplus are usually returned to the policyholders in the form of dividends.

1-3. These are the roles of Lloyd's of London and reciprocal insurance exchanges:

   a. Lloyd's of London is a marketplace that provides the physical and procedural facilities for its members to write insurance. The members are investors who hope to earn a profit from the insurance operations. Lloyd's provides coverage for many unusual or difficult loss exposures and underwrites much of the global marine and aviation insurance.

   b. Reciprocal insurance exchanges consist of a series of private contracts in which subscribers, or members of the group, agree to insure each other. The term "reciprocal" comes from the reciprocity of responsibility of all subscribers to each other. Each member of the reciprocal is both an insured and an insurer.

1-4. A domestic insurer is incorporated within a specific state or, if not incorporated, is formed under the laws of that state. An insurer is said to be operating in its own domiciled state when it is doing business in the state in which it is incorporated or was formed.

1-5. An insurer's state license authorizes it to sell insurance in the state. A license indicates that the insurer has met the state's minimum standards for financial strength, competence, and integrity.

1-6. Some common distribution channels include the Internet, call centers, direct response, group marketing, and financial institutions.

Educational Objective 2

2-1. Insurers earn money by charging insureds a "premium" for the insurance contract. To be able to meet the contract terms through the payment of covered losses and to meet regulatory requirements, insurers invest the portion of premiums that is not needed to pay their operating expenses (called surplus). These investments produce income in the form of interest, dividends, and investment gains—when sold. The return on investments generates additional income to be further invested to pay future covered losses, to expand the insurer's operations, or to be returned to the insurer's investors.

2-2. Meeting customers' needs can often conflict with the profit goal because offering high-quality insurance at a price that the customer can afford may not generate the profit that the insurer needs to attract and retain capital. This is particularly true in certain heavily populated areas where risk-based pricing would not be affordable for insureds. Providing training, operating automated call centers, and maintaining current information technology can also become costly and can conflict with achieving the profit goal in the near term, but in the long term, these related expenses help to create a competitive advantage.

2-3. Being a responsible corporate citizen dictates legal compliance. Additionally, legal compliance promotes the insurer's good reputation in the business community and the insurer's ability to attract capital and customers.

2-4. Diversifying risk is an emerging goal for property-casualty insurers because of the increased catastrophe losses that have occurred over the past decade. The high concentrations of losses in certain geographic areas highlight individual insurers' need to spread risk over a wider geographic area and over multiple types of insurance business, such as property-casualty insurance. Meeting this goal complements the insurer's goals of earning a profit and fulfilling its duty to society.

2-5. Many insurers contribute funds, and sometimes they volunteer employees' time, to medical, educational, and other public service organizations. Additionally, many insurers establish employee benefit plans that provide for the current and future well-being of their employees. Benefits such as medical insurance, disability insurance, retirement plans, employee assistance programs, and numerous others help employees and retirees to use their personal resources to meet their needs and help to minimize the use of public resources. Insurers' participation in philanthropic activities and employee benefits improves employees' job satisfaction and emotional well-being. In addition, these activities help with employee retention and attract qualified candidates to these organizations.

fulfill duty to society by:

Educational Objective 3

3-1. The rapid pace of technology advances makes it difficult for insurers to integrate the latest technological trends into their business processes. The need for historic information on losses and insureds often creates a dependency on core legacy systems, which require ongoing maintenance in addition to integration with new technology. Modern United States culture demands information at the touch of a button, and insurer technology tends to lag behind that of other industries in meeting that demand. These difficulties in meeting customers' technology demands and the competition for funds conflict with an insurer's customer needs and profit goals.

3-2. Large insurers can take advantage of economies of scale and may have more financial resources to update technology or reach additional markets compared with small insurers. Large insurers can invest more in market research and product development than small insurers can. For smaller insurers, these constraints make it difficult to meet their goals.

3-3. Two examples of other constraints that interfere with insurers' achieving their goals are lack of name recognition and a reputation damaged by past problems. Even if an insurer has the expertise and financial resources to achieve its profit goals, insurers new to the insurance market lack the brand recognition of established insurers. If an insurer's reputation is damaged, the insurer may need to develop a concerted campaign to regain customer and public confidence and a plan to manage that image into the future. Internal issues would include ethical decision-making training for all staff, communication of appropriate information to staff for avoidance of morale issues or other negative outcomes, and addressing all internal issues that could cause problems retaining and hiring high-caliber managers and other staff.

3-4. Regulation can extend to the insurance rates and forms insurers use. If filed rate increases are not approved by the applicable regulator, an insurer might not achieve its profit goals. Policy form approval and the time constraints related to the filing process might keep an insurer from fully meeting customers' needs.

3-5. For some insurers, decisions about whether damage was caused by windstorm (which was covered) or flooding (which was not covered) caused an emotional, public outcry following the catastrophic hurricane damage in the 2000s. In some cases, insurers resolved to pay losses that were not covered to curtail damage to their reputations. In this respect, public opinion was a constraint to meeting those insurers' profitability goals.

3-6. In soft cycles, competitive pressure to decrease prices makes it difficult for insurers to achieve their profit goals. Low profits can affect insurers' ability to achieve societal goals. Excessive competition can entice some insurers to bend the rules, making insurers unable to attain their legal and regulatory goals.

3-7. Insurers are increasingly experimenting with multiple distribution systems and channels. Several major companies use both insurance agents and direct sale methods to reach consumers, including Internet and telephone sales. Affinity sales, or selling through special interest groups, represent a growing distribution channel. Additionally, banks are increasingly selling property-casualty insurance to their bank clients. Each distribution system or channel meets the needs of some customers, and each fails to meet the needs of others.

Educational Objective 4

4-1. The two indicators of insurer profitability based on premiums are premium growth issues and the rate of growth that is sustained over time.

4-2. Customer complaints made either directly to the insurer or through the insurance department can indicate the level of customer satisfaction, as can consumer surveys, insurers' retention ratio and lapse ratio, feedback from producers, and *Consumer Reports*.

guage success in meeting customer needs by

4-3. Three sources for measuring an insurer's success or failure in meeting legal requirements are the state insurance department's market conduct regulation; state listings of regulatory actions taken against insurers; and summary information about insurer financial strength and financial ratings provided by financial rating agencies, including any outstanding legal actions involving the organization. The outcomes of such actions are an indicator of how well an insurer meets its legal requirements.

4-4. An insurer's expenditures on loss control activities may go beyond typical efforts in loss control to improve safety conditions for its insureds. Many insurers contribute to associations that do research and raise public concern for safety. Contributions to medical, welfare, and educational institutions and programs are another indication of humanitarian efforts and social responsibility.

Educational Objective 5

5-1. Three core functions that exist within the structure of a typical insurer are marketing and distribution, underwriting, and claims.

5-2. Five supporting functions that exist within the structure of a typical insurer include risk control, premium auditing, actuarial, reinsurance, and information technology.

5-3. Six other common functions include investments, accounting and finance, customer service, legal and compliance, human resources, and special investigation units (SIUs).

Direct Your Learning

Insurance Regulation

Educational Objectives

After learning the content of this assignment, you should be able to:

1. Describe the effect each of the following had on insurance regulation:
   - Paul v. Virginia
   - Sherman Antitrust Act
   - South-Eastern Underwriters Association Decision
   - McCarran-Ferguson Act
   - Insurance Services Office (ISO) and the Attorneys General Lawsuit
   - Gramm-Leach-Bliley Act

2. Explain how insurance regulation protects consumers, contributes to maintaining insurer solvency, and assists in preventing destructive competition.

3. Identify the regulatory activities of state insurance departments and the duties typically performed by state insurance commissioners.

4. Describe the arguments for and against federal regulation of insurance.

5. Describe the licensing requirements for insurers and insurance personnel.

6. Describe the methods that regulators use to maintain the solvency of insurers and to manage insolvencies, and the reasons why insurers become insolvent.

7. Describe the goals of insurance rate regulation, the major types of state rating laws, and the reasons supporting and opposing rate regulation.

8. Explain how the contract language contained in insurance policies is regulated.

9. Explain how the market conduct areas in insurance are regulated and how regulatory activities protect consumers.

Educational Objectives, continued

10. Explain how organizations that act as unofficial regulators affect insurance activities.

Outline

▶ **Evolution of Insurance Regulation**
  A. Paul v. Virginia
  B. Sherman Antitrust Act
  C. South-Eastern Underwriters Association Decision
  D. McCarran-Ferguson Act
  E. ISO and the Attorneys General Lawsuit
  F. Gramm-Leach-Bliley Act

▶ **Reasons for Insurance Regulation**
  A. Protect Consumers
  B. Maintain Insurer Solvency
  C. Prevent Destructive Competition

▶ **Insurance Regulators**
  A. State Insurance Departments
    1. The Insurance Commissioner
    2. State Regulation Funding
  B. The National Association of Insurance Commissioners (NAIC)
    1. Model Laws and Regulations
    2. Accreditation Program
  C. Federal Regulation

▶ **State Versus Federal Insurance Regulation**

▶ **Insurance Regulatory Activities: Licensing Insurers and Insurance Personnel**
  A. Licensing Insurers
    1. Domestic Insurers
    2. Foreign Insurers
    3. Alien Insurers
    4. Nonadmitted Insurers
    5. Risk Retention Groups
  B. Licensing Insurance Personnel
    1. Producers
    2. Claim Representatives
    3. Insurance Consultants

▶ **Insurance Regulatory Activities: Monitoring Insurer Solvency**
  A. Methods to Maintain Solvency
  B. Liquidation of Insolvent Insurers
  C. State Guaranty Funds

  D. Reasons for Insolvency

▶ **Insurance Regulatory Activities: Regulating Insurance Rates**
  A. Insurance Rate Regulation Goals
    1. Adequate
    2. Not Excessive
    3. Not Unfairly Discriminatory
  B. Types of Rating Laws

▶ **Insurance Regulatory Activities: Regulating Insurance Policies**
  A. Legislation
  B. Policy Rules, Regulations, and Guidelines
  C. Courts

▶ **Insurance Regulatory Activities: Market Conduct and Consumer Protection**
  A. Monitoring Market Conduct
    1. Producer Practices
    2. Underwriting Practices
    3. Claim Practices
  B. Market Analysis
  C. Ensuring Consumer Protection

▶ **Unofficial Regulators in Insurance**
  A. Financial Rating Organizations
  B. Insurance Advisory Organizations
  C. Insurance Industry Professional and Trade Associations
  D. Consumer Groups

Reduce the number of Key Words and Phrases that you must review.
SMART Flash Cards contain the Key Words and Phrases and their definitions, allowing you to set aside those cards that you have mastered.

For each assignment, you should define or describe each of the Key Words and Phrases and answer each of the Review and Application Questions.

Educational Objective 1

Describe the effect each of the following had on insurance regulation:

- **Paul v. Virginia**
- **Sherman Antitrust Act**
- **South-Eastern Underwriters Association Decision**
- **McCarran-Ferguson Act**
- **Insurance Services Office (ISO) and the Attorneys General Lawsuit**
- **Gramm-Leach-Bliley Act**

Review Questions

1-1. What role did each of these play in establishing which level of government should regulate insurance?

a.   *Paul v. Virginia*

b.   Sherman Antitrust Act

c.   South-Eastern Underwriters Association decision

    d. McCarran-Ferguson Act

1-2. What changes at Insurance Services Office (ISO) were the result of the settlement of the Attorneys General Lawsuit?

1-3. How does the Gramm-Leach-Bliley (GLB) Act address each of the following issues?

    a. Authority for regulating insurance, banking, and securities functions

    b. Banks' authority to underwrite insurance

c.   Insurance producers' ability to operate in more than one state.

Educational Objective 2

Explain how insurance regulation protects consumers, contributes to maintaining insurer solvency, and assists in preventing destructive competition.

Review Question

2-1. Explain why each of the following is an important goal of insurance regulation.

a.   Protect consumers

b.   Maintain insurer solvency

c.   Prevent destructive competition

Educational Objective 3

Identify the regulatory activities of state insurance departments and the duties typically performed by state insurance commissioners.

Key Words and Phrases

National Association of Insurance Commissioners (NAIC)

Model law

Model regulation

Review Questions

3-1. Identify the types of regulatory activities typically undertaken by state insurance departments.

3-2. Identify the duties of a typical state insurance commissioner.

3-3. In most states, the insurance commissioner is an appointed position; however, many states now have elected commissioners.

a. What arguments do proponents of an elective system cite to support their position?

b. What are the arguments in favor of appointing insurance commissioners?

3-4. Describe the ways in which the National Association of Insurance Commissioners (NAIC) affects the regulation of insurance.

3-5. List the three criteria state insurance departments must meet to satisfy the NAIC's Financial Regulation Standards and to be accredited.

Educational Objective 4
Describe the arguments for and against federal regulation of insurance.

Key Word or Phrase
Systemic risk

Review Question

4-1. Insurance regulation occurs primarily at the state level, but the issue of federal regulation is often raised.

    a.   What arguments have been advanced in favor of federal regulation?

    b.   What arguments have been advanced in favor of continued regulation by the states?

Educational Objective 5
Describe the licensing requirements for insurers and insurance personnel.

Key Words and Phrases
Domestic insurer

Foreign insurer

Alien insurer

Capital stock

Paid-in surplus

Reciprocal insurer

Review Questions

5-1. What requirements must be met to form each of the following?

    a. Domestic stock insurance company

    b. Domestic mutual insurance company

5-2. Explain the difference between an admitted and a nonadmitted insurer.

5-3. Why do some states require claim representatives to be licensed?

Educational Objective 6

Describe the methods that regulators use to maintain the solvency of insurers and to manage insolvencies, and the reasons why insurers become insolvent.

Key Words and Phrases

Insolvency

Guaranty fund

Review Questions

6-1. Describe the typical regulatory solvency requirements for insurers.

6-2. Compare the rehabilitation and liquidation options for insolvent insurers.

6-3. Describe the purpose of state guaranty funds.

6-4. Describe the factors that contribute to insurer insolvencies.

Educational Objective 7

Describe the goals of insurance rate regulation, the major types of state rating laws, and the reasons supporting and opposing rate regulation.

Review Questions

7-1. What are the goals of insurance rate regulation?

7-2. Compare the arguments for prior-approval systems versus competitive rating systems.

7-3. Contrast each of the following pairs as they apply to insurance rates.

   a.   Adequate rates and excessive rates

   b.   Fair discrimination and unfair discrimination

Educational Objective 8
Explain how the contract language contained in insurance policies is regulated.

Review Questions

8-1. How do state insurance regulatory activities by each branch of government affect the wording of insurance policies?

8-2. Explain the purpose of the System for Electronic Rate and Form Filings (SERFF).

Educational Objective 9

Explain how the market conduct areas in insurance are regulated and how regulatory activities protect consumers.

Key Words and Phrases

Good faith claim handling

Bad faith

Review Questions

9-1. Describe the potential consequences for each of these types of unfair practices.

   a. Producer unfair trade practices

b.   Insurer unfair underwriting practices

c.   Insurer unfair claim practices

9-2.   Compare the benefits of market analysis to traditional market conduct examinations.

9-3.   Describe the activities of state insurance departments designed specifically to support consumers.

Educational Objective 10
Explain how organizations that act as unofficial regulators affect insurance activities.

Key Words and Phrases

Mortgagor

Advisory organization

Prospective loss costs

Review Questions

10-1. Explain the purpose of financial rating organizations.

10-2. Explain how financial rating organizations act as unofficial regulators of insurers.

10-3. Explain how advisory organizations function as unofficial regulators of insurers.

10-4. Compare how professional and trade associations act as unofficial regulators in the property-casualty insurance industry.

Answers to Assignment 2 Questions

NOTE: These answers are provided to give students a basic understanding of acceptable types of responses. They often are not the only valid answers and are not intended to provide an exhaustive response to the questions.

Educational Objective 1

1-1.

   a. *Paul v. Virginia* was an 1869 U.S. Supreme Court decision that insurance is not interstate commerce. This decision affirmed state regulation of insurance and denied federal authority to regulate insurance.

   b. This 1890 Congressional act prohibited collusion to gain a monopoly and prevented insurers from banding together to control insurance rates and coverage.

   c. The South-Eastern Underwriters case overruled *Paul v. Virginia* and stated that the federal government had authority to regulate insurance. The South-Eastern Underwriters decision did not, however, immediately create a structure of federal regulation for insurance.

   d. The McCarran-Ferguson Act provided that regulation of insurance would remain with the states and federal antitrust laws would not apply to state control of rate regulation. Federal antitrust laws still applied to boycotts, coercion, and intimidation.

1-2. The Insurance Services Office was reorganized as a result of this settlement. ISO's board was changed to include three insurance company executives, seven noninsurance company executives, and ISO's president as chairperson. Insurer committees have been dissolved and replaced with insurer advisory panels, whose members make recommendations in their areas of expertise.

1-3.

   a. Authority for regulating these businesses is now determined by function. Insurance is regulated by existing state insurance departments, banking is regulated by banking regulators, and securities are regulated by securities regulators.

   b. National banks are prohibited from underwriting insurance through an operating subsidiary, but can arrange for a financial holding company to create an insurance affiliate.

   c. States are compelled to facilitate insurance producers' ability to operate in more than one state. The GLB Act contains a provision that gave states three years to adopt full reciprocal licensing agreements. The National Association of Insurance Commissioners (NAIC) created a Producer Licensing Model Act that requires states to establish either a system of reciprocal producer licensing or uniform licensing standards.

Educational Objective 2

2-1.

   a. Protecting consumers is important because the majority of consumers are not equipped to analyze and understand complicated insurance policies. Insurance regulators are able to review insurance policy forms to ensure that they benefit the consumer. Regulators also protect consumers against fraud and unethical market behavior.

b.   Maintaining insurer solvency is critical in protecting insureds against the risk that insurers will not be able to meet their financial obligations. Insurance consumers, even large commercial customers, may find it difficult to evaluate the financial strength and viability of private insurers.

c.   Underpricing of insurance products to increase market share can lead to destructive competition by depressing price levels in the market as a whole. If prices fall too low, some insurers may become insolvent and some insurers may leave the market, leading to an insurance shortage. Regulators are responsible for determining that insurance rates are high enough to avoid such destructive competition.

Educational Objective 3

3-1.   These are the types of regulatory activities typically undertaken by state insurance departments:

- Licensing insurers
- Licensing producers, claim representatives, and other insurance personnel
- Approving policy forms
- Holding rate hearings and reviewing rate filings
- Evaluating solvency information
- Performing market conduct examinations
- Investigating policyholder complaints
- Rehabilitating or liquidating insolvent insurers
- Issuing cease-and-desist orders
- Fining insurers that violate state law
- Publishing shoppers' guides and other consumer information (in some states)
- Preventing fraud

3-2. These are the duties of a typical state insurance commissioner:

- Overseeing the state insurance department's operation

- Promulgating orders, rules, and regulations necessary to administer insurance laws

- Determining whether to issue business licenses to new insurers, producers, and other insurance entities

- Reviewing insurance pricing and coverage

- Conducting financial and market examinations of insurers

- Holding hearings on insurance issues

- Taking action when insurance laws are violated

- Issuing an annual report on the status of the state's insurance market and insurance department

- Maintaining records of insurance department activities

3-3. These answers list proponents' arguments of an elective system and arguments in favor of appointing insurance commissioners.

a. Proponents of an elective system cite these reasons:

- An appointed insurance commissioner is subject to dismissal, while an elected commissioner is generally in office for a full term.

- An appointed commissioner might continue regulating in the same manner as his or her predecessor when a different approach is required, but an elected commissioner would more likely change the insurance department's stance.

- An appointed commissioner might not be aware of the public's concerns, but an elected commissioner would be keenly aware of the issues important to the public.

- An appointed commissioner might feel inclined to yield to the interests of those responsible for the appointment, while an elected commissioner is not obligated to any particular group or special interest.

b. Proponents of an appointing system cite these reasons:

- An appointed commissioner has no need to campaign or to be unduly influenced by political contributors.

- An appointed commissioner is less likely to be swayed by ill-informed public opinion than an elected one.

- An appointed commissioner is more likely to be perceived as a career government employee interested in regulation than as a politician interested in political advancement.

3-4. The NAIC assists state insurance departments by developing model laws and regulations for enactment by state legislators, by sharing financial information about insurers, and by developing uniform financial statement forms required by all states.

3-5. State insurance departments must meet these three criteria:

- The state's insurance laws and regulations must meet basic standards of NAIC models.

- The state's regulatory methods must be acceptable to the NAIC.

- The state's insurance department practices must be adequate as defined by the NAIC.

Educational Objective 4

4-1.

    a. The major arguments in favor of federal regulation include these:

- Federal regulation can provide regulatory uniformity across all states.

- Federal regulation would be more efficient.

- Federal regulation could attract personnel with a high level of expertise.

- Federal regulation would provide uniformity in the regulation of financial institutions now that banks, which are federally regulated, are involved in insurance.

    b. Those supporting continued regulation by the states present these arguments:

- State regulation is more responsive to local needs.

- The National Association of Insurance Commissioners (NAIC) can facilitate uniformity of state laws.

- State regulation allows for greater opportunities for innovation.

- State regulation is a known entity, and its strengths and weaknesses have already been identified.

- State regulation results in a desirable decentralization of political power.

- State regulation results in multiple eyes looking at an issue.

- State regulation has been responsive in reducing the complexity of regulation.

Educational Objective 5

5-1.

    a. State laws require that domestic stock insurers satisfy certain minimum capital and surplus requirements before a license is granted. Domestic insurers are licensed in the state in which they are incorporated.

    b. Because a mutual insurer has no capital derived from the sale of stock, the minimum requirement applies only to surplus. Most states require mutuals to have an initial surplus equal to the minimum capital and surplus requirements for stock insurers writing the same types of business. Some states also require mutuals to have applications and deposit premiums from a stated minimum number of persons on more than a stated number of separate exposures with aggregate premiums in excess of a stated amount.

5-2. An admitted insurer is licensed by a state insurance department to do business in the insured's home state. A nonadmitted insurer is not licensed in the insured's home state, although it may be an admitted insurer in other states.

5-3. Some states require claim representatives to be licensed to ensure technical competence and to protect consumers from unfair, unethical, and dishonest claim practices.

Educational Objective 6

6-1. These are typical regulatory solvency requirements for insurers:

- Insurers must submit annual and quarterly financial statements to the domestic regulator and the National Association of Insurance Commissioners (NAIC).

- Insurers are required to use the NAIC's Accounting Practices and Procedures Manual and the Annual Statement Blank and Instructions. Any differences in codified accounting practices and a state-permitted practice used by an insurer must be disclosed. Most insurers' financial statements must be audited by a Certified Public Accountant (CPA).

- Insurers must have their reserves approved by an actuary.

- Insurers must perform a risk-based capital calculation (RBC) and report the result to regulators.

- Insurers are required to adhere to state minimum capital and surplus requirements.

- Insurers' investments are restricted by state law. Insurers are required to report their investment valuations to the NAIC Securities Valuation Office (SVO).

- State laws limit the amount of any single insured risk an insurer may write.

- Treatment of reinsurance is governed by the NAIC Credit for Reinsurance Model Law.

6-2. If an insurer falls into insolvency, the insurance commissioner places it into receivership. With proper management, rehabilitation might be possible, and thus the insurer could continue to operate. If the insurer cannot be rehabilitated, it is liquidated according to the state's insurance code. Creditors are usually prioritized according to the NAIC's Uniform Insurers Liquidation Act and receive the failed insurer's assets.

6-3. State guaranty funds pay some of the unpaid claims of insolvent insurers licensed in the particular state. These funds mitigate the effects of insurer insolvencies.

6-4. The factors that contribute to insurer insolvencies include rapid premium growth, inadequate insurance rates, inadequate reserves, excessive expenses, lax controls over managing general agents, uncollectible reinsurance, and fraud. Poor management is at the root of most of these factors.

Educational Objective 7

7-1. The goals of insurance rate regulation are to ensure that rates are adequate, not excessive, and not unfairly discriminatory.

7-2. Proponents of prior-approval systems argue that these systems help maintain insurer solvency through regulatory review of data to analyze the adequacy of rates, help keep rates fair and reasonable, and prevent insurers from raising rates to earn excessive profits. Proponents of competitive rating systems argue that prior-approval systems may cause rates to be inadequate, that competitive rating systems are more flexible and less expensive to administer, and that free market forces lead to reasonable, fair rates.

7-3.

a. Adequate rates generate premiums that provide for payment of all claims and expenses related to those premiums, and are vital in maintaining insurer solvency. Excessive rates allow for unreasonable profits at an unfair cost to consumers.

b. Fair discrimination means that an insurer should charge substantially similar rates for loss exposures that are roughly similar with respect to expected losses and expenses. If similar exposures were to be charged substantially different rates, that would constitute unfair discrimination.

Educational Objective 8

8-1. The nature and content of insurance coverage is controlled by laws that are created and passed by the state legislature. Such legislation may require standard forms or specific wording for policies. Some state laws include readability standards, which may specify the style and form of the contract as well as the size of the print contained in that contract. State law may also require that policy forms be filed and approved by the state insurance department, an executive branch of government. Finally, courts are involved in determining whether certain losses are covered under a contract and in interpreting ambiguous and confusing policy provisions.

8-2. The SERFF system is designed to improve the efficiency of the rate and form filing and approval process and to reduce the time and cost involved in making regulatory filings.

Educational Objective 9

9-1. The potential consequences of using certain unfair practices are these:

a. Producers are subject to fines, penalties, or license revocation if they engage in certain illegal and unethical activities.

b. Regulatory penalties may include a fine per violation and suspension or revocation of the insurer's license. Additionally, unfair underwriting practices can result in an insurer's insolvency.

c. Regulatory penalties may include fines and suspension or revocation of the insurer's license. In addition, legal actions can be filed in the courts by insureds and third-party claimants for the tort of bad faith.

9-2. Market analysis allows regulators to identify general market disruptions, promotes uniform analysis by applying consistent measurements between insurers, and facilitates communication and collaboration among regulators from different states. Traditional market conduct examinations, on the other hand, focus on company-specific issues.

9-3. State insurance departments often assist with complaints about rates or policy cancellations or with consumers' difficulty in finding insurance. To help make consumers more knowledgeable about the cost of insurance, some states publish shoppers' guides and other forms of consumer information.

Educational Objective 10

10-1. Financial rating organizations provide summary information about insurer financial strength in the form of a financial rating, typically a letter grade. Corporate risk managers, independent insurance producers, and consumers consult these ratings when selecting an insurer.

10-2. Insurers whose financial ratings decline can find it difficult to attract and retain customers. Many corporate and public entity risk managers, as well as contractors, are required to choose insurers with ratings above a certain grade level. Therefore, insurers strive to attain and maintain good financial ratings.

10-3. By developing rate information and standard insurance forms, advisory organizations provide uniformity, leading to consistent practices among insurers that benefit consumers and regulators, as well as the insurers themselves.

10-4. Professional associations provide leadership and education for their members. They also contribute to establishing standards and practices for various groups of professionals employed throughout the industry. Trade associations are often involved in activities to influence the development of legislation and regulation that will affect either a segment of the insurance industry or the entire industry. These associations also inform their members of changes in laws and regulations.

Direct Your Learning

Insurance Marketing and Distribution

Educational Objectives

After learning the content of this assignment, you should be able to:

1. Describe the following attributes of the competitive property-casualty insurance marketplace: distinguishing characteristics of insurance customers, insurer marketing differentiations, and unique factors in the insurance marketplace.

2. Explain how typical insurer marketing activities are performed and why they are performed.

3. Describe the main types of insurance distribution systems and channels, including the principal characteristics that distinguish one distribution system from another.

4. Describe the functions performed by insurance producers.

5. Describe the key factors an insurer should evaluate during the distribution-system and distribution-channel selection process.

Outline

▶ **Property-Casualty Insurance Marketplace**

A. Characteristics of Property-Casualty Insurance Customers
   1. Individuals
   2. Small Business
   3. Middle Markets
   4. National Accounts

B. Property-Casualty Insurer Marketing Differentiations
   1. Customer Focus
   2. Products and Services
   3. Size
   4. Geographic Area
   5. Distribution System

C. Unique Factors that Shape the Insurance Marketplace
   1. Economic Forces
   2. Regulatory Controls
   3. Demands for Technology
   4. Underwriting Cycles
   5. Unanticipated Catastrophic Losses

▶ **Insurer Marketing Activities**

A. Marketing Research
   1. Market Research Methods
   2. Market Segmentation

B. Market Development

C. Marketing Information

D. Marketing Planning

E. Product Development

F. Advertising and Promotion

G. Customer and Public Relations

H. Sales Fulfillment

▶ **Insurance Distributions Systems and Channels**

A. Independent Agency and Brokerage Marketing Systems
   1. Independent Agents and Brokers
   2. National and Regional Brokers
   3. Independent Agent Networks
   4. Managing General Agents (MGAs)
   5. Surplus Lines Brokers

B. Exclusive Agency Marketing System

C. Direct Writer Marketing System

D. Distribution Channels
   1. Internet
   2. Call Centers
   3. Direct Response
   4. Group Marketing
   5. Financial Institutions

E. Mixed Marketing System

▶ **Functions of Insurance Producers**

A. Prospecting

B. Risk Management Review
   1. Individual or Family
   2. Businesses

C. Sales

D. Policy Issuance

E. Premium Collection

F. Customer Service

G. Claim Handling

H. Consulting

▶ **Distribution System and Channel Selection for Insurance Marketing**

A. Customers' Needs and Characteristics

B. Insurer's Profile
   1. Insurer Strategies and Goals
   2. Insurer Strengths
   3. Existing and Target Markets
   4. Geographic Location
   5. Degree of Control Required

Actively capture information by using the open space in the SMART Review Notes to write out key concepts. Putting information into your own words is an effective way to push that information into your memory.

For each assignment, you should define or describe each of the Key Words and Phrases and answer each of the Review and Application Questions.

Educational Objective 1

Describe the following attributes of the competitive property-casualty insurance marketplace: distinguishing characteristics of insurance customers, insurer marketing differentiations, and unique factors in the insurance marketplace.

Key Words and Phrases

Producer

Market intelligence

Underwriting cycle

Review Questions

1-1.   List the five characteristics that distinguish types of insurance customers.

1-2.   Summarize how the insurance needs of small business can be covered.

1-3. How can market intelligence help an insurer improve its customer focus?

1-4. What factors influence an insurer's decision regarding the geographic area it serves?

1-5. Describe economic influences on property-casualty insurers' operations.

Educational Objective 2
Explain how typical insurer marketing activities are performed and why they are performed.

Key Words and Phrases
Focus group

Predictive analytics

Market segmentation

Target marketing

Niche marketing

Review Questions

2-1. Contrast primary data and secondary data used for insurer market research.

2-2. Explain how predictive analytics are used in market research.

2-3. Describe four common bases of market segmentation.

2-4. Describe two major types of marketing information systems.

2-5. Before introducing a new insurance product or service, an insurer completes a comprehensive marketing plan. Describe the function of this plan.

2-6. Describe activities of the insurer customer relations function.

Educational Objective 3

Describe the main types of insurance distribution systems and channels, including the principal characteristics that distinguish one distribution system from another.

Key Words and Phrases

Distribution system

Agency expiration list

Countersignature laws

▶▶

Managing general agent (MGA)

Direct response distribution channel

Affinity marketing

Review Questions

3-1. Why is ownership of expiration lists an advantage to an independent agency?

3-2. What are the benefits an independent agent network can offer to its members?

3-3. Surplus lines brokers have access to insurers that have the capacity to provide insurance for specific customers or exposures that might otherwise be uninsurable. List five such customers or exposures.

Educational Objective 4

Describe the functions performed by insurance producers.

Key Words and Phrases

Cold canvass

Loss run

Agency bill

Direct bill

Review Questions

4-1.   Name six methods producers use to locate prospective clients.

4-2. Describe the types of information included in a loss run that may be of use to a producer.

4-3. Describe three widely used methods used to transfer premiums to insurers in the agency bill process.

4-4. Describe two advantages of using qualified producers to handle claims.

Educational Objective 5

Describe the key factors an insurer should evaluate during the distribution-system and distribution-channel selection process.

Review Questions

5-1. What factors must an insurer evaluate relating to its profile when selecting distribution systems and channels?

5-2.   How can assessment of its internal strengths and weaknesses help an insurer in the selection of distribution systems and channels?

5-3.   What considerations relating to existing markets might an insurer evaluate during the process of selecting distribution systems and channels?

Answers to Assignment 3 Questions

NOTE: These answers are provided to give students a basic understanding of acceptable types of responses. They often are not the only valid answers and are not intended to provide an exhaustive response to the questions.

Educational Objective 1

1-1. The characteristics that distinguish types of insurance customers are insurance needs, knowledge of the insurance markets, methods of accessing the insurance market, negotiating ability, and access to alternative risk financing measures.

1-2. The insurance needs of small businesses can usually be covered by a limited number of commercial insurance policies, such as a businessowners policy, a workers compensation policy, and commercial auto policies.

1-3. Market intelligence provides insurers with information that is relevant to understanding customers' current and future needs, preferences, attitudes, and behaviors. This depth of understanding leads to better customer interaction through an intensified customer-market view. Through market intelligence, the insurer understands where its insurance offer fits and discovers untapped or underserved potential markets.

1-4. An insurer's decision regarding geographic area is based on its size, its level of expertise in writing coverage in broader geographic areas, the level of competition in those areas, and its customer focus. An insurer that chooses a regional area for operation can more narrowly focus its marketing intelligence to address customers' insurance needs in the smaller area. In contrast, writing insurance nationally or internationally requires substantially more marketing intelligence to understand customers and successfully meet a wider range of insurance needs.

1-5. Inflation is a factor in increasing the costs of losses and the costs of an insurer's operations. The availability of reinsurance influences the price and the cost of insurer operations. Investment earnings frequently offset high losses and rising costs. When investment earnings are diminished or the prospect of catastrophe losses increase, insurers must raise premiums to sustain risk-appropriate rates of return.

Educational Objective 2

2-1. Secondary data are data that have been collected by other parties and are therefore immediately available at little or no cost. Many research questions can be answered at minimal expense from secondary data. Because primary data are collected by the insurer, they are more costly to acquire; however, these data address issues specific to the market research project.

2-2. Most predictive models generate a score, with the higher score indicating a higher likelihood that the given behavior or event will occur. Predictive scores are typically used to measure the risk or opportunity associated with a specific customer or transaction. These evaluations assess the relationships between many variables to estimate risk or response.

2-3. Marketers commonly use four bases of segmentation, among others:

- Behavioristic segmentation—the division of a total consumer market by purchase behavior

- Geographic segmentation—the division of markets by geographic units

- Demographic segmentation—the division of markets based on demographic variables, such as age, gender, education, occupation, ethnicity, income, family size, and family life cycle

- Psychographic segmentation—the division of markets by individuals' values, personalities, attitudes, and lifestyles

2-4. Marketing information is divided into two major types of systems:

- The internal accounting system provides report and analysis capability based on transactions associated with sales activity. Much of the essential information on production, retention, and policies in force is available as a byproduct of the systems that keep track of commissions and billings.

- The market monitor system provides intelligence about the external environment to inform senior management about important developments and changing conditions. Customers and producers are monitored to determine their satisfaction levels with the service they receive from the insurer, and the resulting information helps the insurer shape decisions related to growth and profitability strategies. The market monitor also maintains competitive intelligence and benchmark studies of competitors.

2-5. A comprehensive marketing plan identifies the product or service to be promoted and the customers to be targeted, and it details the resources and strategies that will be used to create, price, promote, and sell the product or service.

2-6. The customer relations function manages communications with individual customers from the home office, ensuring that all written communications seen by customers are understandable and consistent in quality and tone. It provides a forum for communications to the insurer initiated by customers, including complaints, suggestions, and questions, and may respond to state insurance departments in relation to consumer complaints about the insurer. The customer relations function also provides management with low-cost, high-value information about the evolving wants and needs of policyholders.

Educational Objective 3

3-1. Ownership of expiration lists is an agency's most valuable asset. If an insurer ceases to do business with the agency, the agency has the right to continue doing business with its existing customers by selling them insurance with another insurer.

3-2. The benefits an independent agent network can offer its members include these:

- Obtaining access to an increased number of insurers
- Meeting countersignature law requirements for businesses in multiple states
- Combining premium volume to meet insurer requirements for profit-sharing
- Generating additional sales income
- Receiving preferred agency contracts
- Facilitating agency succession planning
- Providing expertise in risk management services
- Offering expertise in financial planning services
- Enabling resource sharing and expense reduction
- Increasing market share

3-3. Surplus lines brokers have access to insurers that have the capacity to provide insurance for these specific customers or exposures:

- A customer that requires high limits of insurance
- A customer that requires unusually broad or specialized coverage
- An unusual or a unique loss exposure
- Loss exposures requiring a tailored insurance program
- An unfavorable loss exposure, such as a poor claim history or difficult-to-treat exposures

Educational Objective 4

4-1. Prospects can be located using several methods:

- Referrals from present clients
- Referrals from strategic partners, such as financial institutions and real estate brokers
- Advertising in multimedia and direct mail
- Interactive Web sites
- Telephone solicitations
- Cold canvass

4-2. Loss runs include, at a minimum, lists of losses and their total cost. More comprehensive loss runs provide details that can lead to additional questions and suggest areas of risk management improvement.

4-3. Businesses that are agency billed commonly use these three methods of transmitting premiums to insurers:

- Item basis—The premium (less commission) is forwarded to the insurer when the producer collects it or when it becomes due. The producer is usually not required to pay the insurer until the premium has been collected.

- Statement basis—The insurer sends a statement to the producer showing the premiums that are due. The producer is obligated to pay the premiums indicated as due or to show that the statement is in error.

- Account current basis—The producer periodically prepares a statement showing the premiums due to the insurer, after deducting appropriate commissions, and transmits that amount to the insurer. The producer must pay the insurer when the premium is due, as specified in the agency contract, even if the policyholders have not paid the producer.

4-4. Claim handling by qualified producers offers two major advantages: quicker service to policyholders and lower loss adjustment expenses to the insurer.

Educational Objective 5

5-1. An insurer must evaluate these factors relating to its profile:

- Its strategies and goals
- Its strengths
- Its existing and target markets
- Its geographic location
- Its desired or required degree of control over producers

5-2. Determining where its strengths lie, an insurer selects distribution systems and channels that maximize its opportunities to capture market share and minimize its weaknesses.

5-3. The insurer should consider the characteristics of its existing book of business. If agents or brokers own the expirations for current accounts, the insurer must either give up that business and start over or purchase the expirations from producers. Either option might be expensive, depending on the quality of the existing business. The insurer should also consider the possibility that a change in distribution systems and channels could disrupt communication channels, causing changes in communication patterns that can result in policyholder dissatisfaction and lost accounts.

Direct Your Learning

The Underwriting Function

Educational Objectives

After learning the content of this assignment, you should be able to:

1. Describe the purpose of underwriting.

2. Describe the underwriting activities typically performed by line and staff underwriters.

3. Describe the importance of compliance with underwriting authority in individual account selection.

4. Describe the constraining factors considered in the establishment of underwriting policy.

5. Describe the purposes that underwriting guidelines and underwriting audits serve.

6. Describe the steps in the underwriting process.

7. Explain how an insurer's underwriting results are measured and how financial measures can be distorted.

Outline

▶ **Purpose of Underwriting**
  A. Guarding Against Adverse Selection
  B. Ensuring Adequate Policyholders' Surplus
  C. Enforcing Underwriting Guidelines

▶ **Underwriting Activities**
  A. Line Underwriting Activities
    1. Select Insureds
    2. Classify and Price Accounts
    3. Recommend or Provide Coverage
    4. Manage a Book of Business
    5. Support Producers and Customers
    6. Coordinate With Marketing Efforts
  B. Staff Underwriting Activities
    1. Research the Market
    2. Formulate Underwriting Policy
    3. Revise Underwriting Guidelines
    4. Evaluate Loss Experience
    5. Research and Develop Coverage Forms
    6. Review and Revise Pricing Plans
    7. Arrange Treaty Reinsurance
    8. Assist Others With Complex Accounts
    9. Conduct Underwriting Audits
    10. Participate in Industry Associations
    11. Conduct Education and Training

▶ **Underwriting Authority**

▶ **Constraints in Establishing Underwriting Policy**
  A. Financial Capacity
  B. Regulation
  C. Personnel
  D. Reinsurance

▶ **Implementing Underwriting Policy**
  A. Purposes of Underwriting Guidelines
    1. Provide for Structured Decisions
    2. Ensure Uniformity and Consistency
    3. Synthesize Insights and Experience
    4. Distinguish Between Routine and Nonroutine Decisions
    5. Avoid Duplication of Efforts

  6. Ensure Adherence to Reinsurance Treaties and Planned Rate Levels
    7. Support Policy Preparation and Compliance
    8. Provide a Basis for Predictive Models
  B. Purposes of Underwriting Audits

▶ **Underwriting Process**
  A. Evaluate the Submission
    1. Weigh the Need for Information
    2. Gather the Necessary Information
  B. Develop Underwriting Alternatives
    1. Require Risk Control Measures
    2. Change Insurance Rates, Rating Plans, or Policy Limits
    3. Amend Policy Terms and Conditions
    4. Use Facultative Reinsurance
  C. Select an Underwriting Alternative
  D. Determine an Appropriate Premium
  E. Implement the Underwriting Decision
  F. Monitor the Underwriting Decisions
    1. Monitor Individual Policies
    2. Monitor Books of Business

▶ **Measuring Underwriting Results**
  A. Financial Measures
    1. Distortions Created by Changes in Premium Volume
    2. Distortions Created by Major Catastrophic Losses
    3. Distortions Created by Delays in Loss Reporting and Loss Development
    4. Distortions Created by Underwriting Cycle
  B. Nonfinancial Measures
    1. Selection
    2. Product or Line of Business Mix
    3. Pricing
    4. Accommodated Accounts
    5. Retention Ratio
    6. Hit Ratio
    7. Service to Producers
    8. Premium to Underwriter

Use the SMART Online Practice Exams to test your understanding of the course material. You can review questions over a single assignment or multiple assignments, or you can take an exam over the entire course.

For each assignment, you should define or describe each of the Key Words and Phrases and answer each of the Review and Application Questions.

Educational Objective 1
Describe the purpose of underwriting.

Key Words and Phrases

Policyholders' surplus

Capacity

Underwriting authority

Review Questions

1-1. Describe the approaches underwriters take to minimize the effects of adverse selection.

1-2. Describe the approaches underwriters take to ensure the adequacy of policy-holders' surplus.

1-3. Describe the approaches underwriters take to ensure that the policies of accepted applicants adhere to underwriting guidelines.

Educational Objective 2
Describe the underwriting activities typically performed by line and staff underwriters.

Key Words and Phrases

Line underwriter

Staff underwriter

Manuscript policy

Underwriting policy (underwriting philosophy)

Loss development

Trending

Treaty reinsurance

Underwriting audit

Review Questions

2-1. Distinguish between the activities of line underwriters and those of staff underwriters.

2-2. Describe the goals of effective account selection by line underwriters.

2-3. Some underwriting guides contain systematic instructions for handling particular classes of commercial accounts. Describe the instructions such guides might include.

2-4. Explain how staff underwriters are involved in the development of coverage forms.

Educational Objective 3

Describe the importance of compliance with underwriting authority in individual account selection.

Review Questions

3-1. Explain why it is important that underwriters operate within their assigned levels of underwriting authority.

3-2. Describe how insurers communicate underwriting authority through underwriting guidelines.

Educational Objective 4

Describe the constraining factors considered in the establishment of underwriting policy.

Key Words and Phrases

Premium-to-surplus ratio or capacity ratio

Statutory accounting principles (SAP)

Return on equity (ROE)

Market conduct examination

Review Questions

4-1. Describe the components of an insurer's financial capacity.

4-2. Explain how rapid premium growth can cause insurers to experience excessive premium-to-surplus ratios.

4-3. Identify four ways that regulation may affect underwriting policy.

4-4. Describe the types of underlying insurance forms that may concern reinsurers.

Educational Objective 5
Describe the purposes that underwriting guidelines and underwriting audits serve.

Key Word or Phrase

Predictive modeling

Review Questions

5-1.   Explain how underwriting guidelines provide a structure for underwriting decisions.

5-2.   Contrast routine underwriting decisions with nonroutine underwriting decisions.

5-3.   Explain how compliance with underwriting guidelines ensures adherence to reinsurance treaty limitations.

5-4. Describe the potential advantages of using predictive modeling in making underwriting decisions.

5-5. Explain how underwriting audits provide staff underwriters with information on the effectiveness of existing underwriting guidelines.

Educational Objective 6
Describe the steps in the underwriting process.

Key Words and Phrases

Underwriter

Underwriting submission

Expert systems, or knowledge-based systems

Loss exposure

Hazard

Information efficiency

Application

Counteroffer

(a) rated classification

Estimated loss potentials (ELP)

Experience rating

Schedule rating

Retrospective rating

Facultative reinsurance

Account underwriting

Unfair trade practices

Binder

Certificate of insurance

Review Questions

6-1. What are the steps in the underwriting process?

6-2. List five principal sources of underwriting information.

6-3. What four major modifications might an underwriter recommend to make a submission more acceptable?

6-4. What factors beyond the content of a submission itself must an underwriter consider before selecting an underwriting alternative?

6-5. Why is it important for the underwriter to correctly classify each loss exposure in a submission when determining the appropriate premium?

6-6. Why should underwriters monitor underwriting results of territories or geographic areas?

Application Question

6-7. Rachel is a personal insurance underwriter for Acme Insurance Company, an insurer using the independent agency system. One day, she receives a request for automobile insurance from a client of one of Acme's newly appointed agents. The applicant is a twenty-four-year-old single male who was previously insured by a direct writer. The application indicates no accidents or traffic violations in the previous three-year period. Rachel suspects that the field underwriting may have been inadequate and believes that additional information is needed because the applicant is new business for the company.

    a.   List the external and internal sources of underwriting information that Rachel might use to reach her decision.

    b.   What factors will determine how much and what kinds of information Rachel might request?

Educational Objective 7
Explain how an insurer's underwriting results are measured and how financial measures can be distorted.

Key Words and Phrases

Combined ratio

Production underwriting

Hit ratio

Review Questions

7-1. What do insurers use the combined ratio to measure?

7-2. What would an underwriter conclude about each of the following combined ratios?

    a.   A combined ratio of exactly 100 percent

    b.   A combined ratio of greater than 100 percent

    c.   A combined ratio of less than 100 percent

7-3. An insurer decides to make its underwriting criteria more restrictive. Explain how this change affects premium volume and the insurer's combined ratio.

7-4. List some aspects of an insurer's operations that are affected by the underwriting cycle.

7-5. How do pricing standards benefit insurers?

Application Question

7-6. Insurance Company has incurred underwriting expenses of $5 million, incurred losses and loss adjustment expenses of $14 million, net written premiums of $25 million, and earned premiums of $20 million.

    a.   Determine Insurance Company's trade-basis combined ratio.

    b.   What does this ratio indicate regarding Insurance Company's use of its premium dollars?

Answers to Assignment 4 Questions

NOTE: These answers are provided to give students a basic understanding of acceptable types of responses. They often are not the only valid answers and are not intended to provide an exhaustive response to the questions.

Educational Objective 1

1-1. To minimize the effects of adverse selection, underwriters carefully select the applicants whose loss exposures they are willing to insure, charge premiums that accurately reflect the loss exposures for those applicants they select, and monitor applications and books of business for unusual patterns of policy growth or loss.

1-2. Underwriters ensure the adequacy of policyholders' surplus by adhering to underwriting guidelines, making certain that all loss exposures are correctly identified, and charging adequate premiums for the applications that are accepted.

1-3. If loss exposures, risks, or policy limits on an application exceed an underwriter's authority, he or she will seek approval through supervisory and management ranks within the underwriting department.

Educational Objective 2

2-1. Line underwriters evaluate individual accounts for acceptability and execute underwriting policy by following practices and procedures outlined by staff underwriters. Staff underwriters work closely with underwriting management to perform activities essential for profitable risk selection.

2-2. Effective account selection by line underwriters is essential to attaining these goals:

- Avoiding adverse selection

- Charging adequate premiums for accounts with a higher-than-average chance of loss

- Selecting better-than-average accounts for which the premium charged will be more than adequate

- Rationing an insurer's available capacity to obtain an optimum spread of loss exposures by location, class, size of risk, and line of business

2-3. Such underwriting guides identify specific hazards to evaluate, alternatives to consider, criteria to use when making the final decision, ways to implement the decision, and methods to monitor the decision. The guides may also provide pricing instructions and reinsurance-related information.

2-4. Staff underwriters work cooperatively with the actuarial and legal departments to develop new coverages and modify existing coverage forms developed by advisory organizations.

Educational Objective 3

3-1. Compliance with levels of authority ensures that the insurer accepts applicants within its underwriting policy.

3-2. A notation next to a specific classification in the underwriting guide might indicate that a senior underwriter must review and approve an application from that classification before it is processed further. Depending on the concerns that underwriting management places on a classification, underwriting approval might be required from the line underwriter's branch manager or a staff underwriter at the home office.

Educational Objective 4

4-1. An insurer's financial capacity refers to the relationship between premiums written and the size of the policyholders' surplus or the insurer's net worth.

4-2. Rapid premium growth results in a reduction in policyholders' surplus to pay for expenses generated by that growth, due to conservative statutory accounting principles used in insurance. This constraint often precludes premium expansion unless the insurer purchases reinsurance or obtains more capital.

4-3. Regulation may affect underwriting policy in these ways:

- Insurers must be licensed to write insurance in each state in which they do business.

- Rates, rules, and forms must be filed with state regulators.

- Underwriting guidelines are required to be filed in some states.

- If consumer groups believe that the insurance industry has not adequately served certain geographic areas, regulatory focus on insurance availability can lead to requirements to extend coverage to loss exposures that an insurer might otherwise not write.

4-4. Reinsurers may expressly exclude reinsurance coverage for loss exposures covered by underlying manuscript forms developed for a particular insured or covered by underlying forms developed independently of an advisory organization.

Educational Objective 5

5-1. Underwriting guidelines provide a structure for underwriting decisions by identifying the major considerations underwriters should evaluate for each type of insurance the insurer writes.

5-2. Routine decisions are those for which the line underwriter clearly has decision-making authority according to the underwriting guidelines. Nonroutine decisions involve submissions that fall outside the underwriter's authority.

5-3. Compliance with underwriting guidelines ensures that coverage limits and accepted loss exposures will not exceed the insurer's treaty reinsurance, because staff underwriters reflect those treaty limitations in the guidelines.

5-4. Predictive modeling can provide a consistent way to review individual applications that improves the overall profitability of a book of business. It can also help in managing a large book of business for which conducting an in-depth underwriting review on every account would be too costly.

5-5. Underwriting guidelines that are not being following may be either outdated or considered unrealistic, which could indicate that a critical review for updates is required.

Educational Objective 6

6-1. The underwriting process entails these six steps:

    a.   Evaluate the submission

    b.   Develop underwriting alternatives

    c.   Select an underwriting alternative

    d.   Determine an appropriate premium

    e.   Implement the underwriting decision

    f.   Monitor underwriting decisions

6-2. Any five of these are principal sources of underwriting information: producers, insurance applications, inspection reports, government records, financial rating services, loss data, field marketing personnel, premium auditors, claim files, production records, and consultants' reports.

6-3. An underwriter may suggest these modifications to a submission:

- Require loss control measures

- Change insurance rates, rating plans, or policy limits

- Amend policy terms and conditions

- Use facultative reinsurance

6-4. The underwriter must consider these factors before selecting an alternative:

- Underwriting authority—Whether the underwriter has the necessary underwriting authority

- Supporting business—Whether an otherwise marginal submission might be acceptable if the other insurance components of the applicant's account—the supporting business—are desirable

- Mix of business—Whether accepting the application supports the insurer's goals for mix of business

- Producer relationships—Whether the relationship between the underwriter and the producer is based on mutually shared goals

- Regulatory restrictions—Whether any state regulations restrict underwriters' ability to accept or renew business, and whether any federal and state privacy laws restrict the type and the amount of information about an applicant that an underwriter can obtain

6-5. Accurate classification ensures a pooling of loss exposures whose expected loss frequency and loss severity are similar. Misclassification can produce adverse results, including insufficient premium to cover losses and expenses, inability to sell policies because prices are higher than competitors' prices, and charges that the insurer has violated regulations prohibiting unfair trade practices.

6-6. Monitoring territorial underwriting results can help the insurer to target areas for future agency appointments in profitable regions. Poor results could indicate areas from which the insurer might withdraw or in which the insurer might raise rates, if permitted by regulators.

6-7. These answers apply to questions regarding Rachel's underwriting decision:

a. Beyond the application, Rachel can use these sources to obtain additional underwriting information (other possible sources do not relate directly to personal auto insurance):

- The producer may have firsthand knowledge of the applicant and may know the applicant's reputation in the community.

- Government records include motor vehicle reports, criminal court records, and civil court records. Motor vehicle records (MVRs) are a fundamental information source for auto underwriting.

- Production records of individual producers, indicating loss ratio, premium volume, mix of business, amount of supporting business, length of service, and industry experience, help underwriters make decisions about the quality of the applicants that the producer is submitting. In personal auto underwriting, for example, the mix of business indicates whether a particular producer is submitting an inordinately large percentage of young drivers or drivers with poor driving records.

b. The amount of time required to receive the information and the cost to acquire the information are important considerations. Underwriters must balance the degree of hazard with how much information is needed and the cost to acquire the information.

Educational Objective 7

7-1. Insurers use the combined ratio to measure the success of underwriting activities.

7-2. An underwriter would reach these conclusions about the combined ratios:

a. Exactly 100 percent—Every premium dollar is being used to pay claims and cover operating costs, with nothing remaining for insurer profit.

b. Greater than 100 percent—An underwriting loss occurs; more dollars are being paid out than are being taken in as premiums.

c. Less than 100 percent—An underwriting profit occurs; not all premium dollars taken in are being used for claims and expenses.

7-3. An insurer that becomes more restrictive in its underwriting criteria will usually see a reduction in premiums written. Because incurred losses remain outstanding from the prior period that had a less restrictive underwriting policy, the loss ratio component of the combined ratio will likely deteriorate. With this reduction in premiums written, the expense ratio will increase, even though the insurer's underwriting expenses might have remained relatively unchanged.

7-4. The underwriting cycle affects premium levels, capital allocation strategies, investment strategies, and insurer profitability.

7-5. Pricing standards enable insurers to determine levels of premium adequacy by comparing premiums charged to the established pricing standards. Insurers also track the extent to which their underwriters deviate from the insurer's established pricing for specific classifications. This information might be useful in determining the extent to which the underwriter's book of business is underpriced or overpriced and where pricing adjustments might be made, should market conditions change.

7-6.   These answers are based on Insurance Company's financial data:

a.   Insurance Company's trade basis combined ratio would be calculated:

$$\frac{\text{Incurred losses and loss adjustment expenses}}{\text{Earned premiums}} + \frac{\text{Incurred underwriting expenses}}{\text{Net written premiums}}$$

$$= \frac{14,000,000}{20,000,000} + \frac{5,000,000}{25,000,000}$$

$$= 0.70 + 0.20 = 0.90 \text{ or } 90\%.$$

b.   The ratio indicates that Insurance Company has an underwriting profit because not all of its premium dollars are being used for claims and expenses.

Direct Your Learning

Underwriting Property and Liability Insurance

Educational Objectives

After learning the content of this assignment, you should be able to:

1. Describe in detail each of the COPE factors used to evaluate property loss exposures.

2. Explain how insurable interest, policy provisions for valuing losses, and insurance to value affect a loss payment amount under property insurance.

3. Explain how underwriters use policy amount, amount subject, normal loss expectancy (NLE), probable maximum loss (PML), and maximum foreseeable loss (MFL) to measure potential loss severity.

4. Describe the underwriting considerations for business income and extra expense coverage.

5. Describe the underwriting considerations and risk control techniques associated with employee dishonesty and crimes committed by others.

6. Describe the loss exposures and the underwriting considerations for commercial general liability insurance.

7. Describe the underwriting considerations for personal and commercial auto insurance.

8. Describe the underwriting considerations for workers compensation insurance.

9. Describe the underwriting considerations for umbrella and excess liability insurance.

Outline

▶ **Underwriting Property Insurance Using the COPE Model**
   A. Construction
      1. Construction Classes
      2. Construction Materials
      3. Building Age
      4. Building Height
      5. Fire Divisions
      6. Building Openings
      7. Building Codes
   B. Occupancy
      1. Occupancy Categories
      2. Characteristics of Contents
      3. Occupancy Hazards
   C. Protection
      1. Public Fire Protection
      2. Private Fire Protection: Prevention
      3. Private Fire Protection: Detection
      4. Private Fire Protection: Suppression
   D. External Exposure
      1. Single-Occupancy Loss Exposures
      2. Multiple-Occupancy Loss Exposures

▶ **Property Policy Provision Underwriting Considerations**
   A. Insurable Interest
   B. Policy Provisions for Valuing Losses
   C. Insurance to Value

▶ **Measures of Potential Loss Severity**
   A. Policy Amount
   B. Amount Subject
   C. Normal Loss Expectancy
   D. Probable Maximum Loss
   E. Maximum Foreseeable Loss

▶ **Underwriting Business Income and Extra Expense Coverage**
   A. Probable Maximum Loss
   B. Factors Affecting the Period of Interruption
      1. Rebuilding Time
      2. Seasonality
      3. Bottlenecks
      4. Computer Systems
      5. Long Production Processes
      6. Availability of Substitutes
      7. Business Continuity and Disaster Recovery Planning

▶ **Underwriting Commercial Crime Insurance**
   A. Employee Dishonesty
      1. Underwriting Employee Dishonesty Loss Exposures
      2. Controlling Employee Dishonesty Losses
   B. Crimes Committed by Others
      1. Underwriting Crimes Committed by Others Loss Exposures
      2. Controlling Crime Committed by Others Loss Exposures

▶ **Underwriting Commercial General Liability Insurance**
   A. Premises and Operations Liability Underwriting Considerations
      1. Extent of Public Exposure
      2. Physical Hazards
      3. Contractors and Subcontractors
   B. Products and Completed Operations Liability Underwriting Considerations
      1. Sources of Products Liability
      2. Underwriting Products Liability Loss Exposures
      3. Underwriting Completed Operations Loss Exposures
   C. Personal and Advertising Injury Liability Underwriting Considerations
   D. Premises Medical Payments Liability Underwriting Considerations

▶ **Underwriting Personal and Commercial Auto Insurance**
   A. Personal Auto Underwriting Considerations
      1. Age of Operator
      2. Age and Type of Auto
      3. Auto Use
      4. Driving Record
      5. Territory

The SMART Online Practice Exams product contains a final practice exam. You should take this exam only when you have completed your study of the entire course. It will be your best indicator of how well prepared you are.

      6. Gender and Marital Status

      7. Occupation

      8. Personal Characteristics

      9. Physical Condition of Driver

      10. Safety Equipment

   B. Commercial Auto Underwriting Considerations

      1. Vehicle Weight and Type

      2. Vehicle Use

      3. Radius of Operation

      4. Special Industry Classifications

   C. Underwriting Use of Risk Control Services

      1. Risk Control Reports

      2. Fleet Safety Programs

▶ **Underwriting Workers Compensation Insurance**

   A. Underwriting Guidelines for Individual Classes and Applicants

      1. Experience Modification Factor

      2. Temporary and Seasonal Employees

      3. Subcontractors

      4. Maritime Occupations

      5. Relative Premium Size

      6. Employee Concentration

   B. Management Attitude and Capability

   C. On-Premises Hazards

      1. Housekeeping

      2. Maintenance

      3. Occupational Disease

      4. Cumulative Trauma Injuries

      5. Analysis of On-Premises Hazards

   D. Off-Premises Hazards

▶ **Underwriting Umbrella and Excess Liability Insurance**

   A. Umbrella and Excess Liability Insurance

   B. Underwriting the Risk

   C. Underwriting the Underlying Policies

   D. Underwriting the Insurer

For each assignment, you should define or describe each of the Key Words and Phrases and answer each of the Review and Application Questions.

Educational Objective 1
Describe in detail each of the COPE factors used to evaluate property loss exposures.

Key Words and Phrases

Frame construction

Joisted masonry construction

Mill construction

Noncombustible construction

Masonry noncombustible construction

Modified fire-resistive construction

Fire-resistive construction

Fuel load (fire load)

Fire division

Fire wall

Parapet

Building codes

Occupancy

Special hazards of the class

Special hazards of the risk

Protection

Public fire protection

Local fire alarm system

Central station system

Wet pipe sprinkler systems

Dry pipe sprinkler systems

Pre-action sprinkler systems

Deluge sprinkler system

Fire brigade

External exposure

Review Questions

1-1. Compare the principal features of fire-resistive construction with those of non-combustible construction.

1-2. How does interior finish affect underwriting acceptability for fire insurance?

1-3. Explain why the age of a building affects fire underwriting.

1-4. Why are high-rise buildings a concern to fire underwriters?

1-5. What are the principal ignition sources associated with the occupancy of a building?

1-6. Describe the factors considered in the determination of a community's public protection classification.

1-7. Describe the risk control measures that may be used to reduce external exposures.

Application Questions

1-8. Charles has contracted with Ed to construct a large shopping complex on a fifty-acre site in a rural community. They ask an insurance producer to set up a meeting with an insurance company underwriter before the start of construction to seek suggestions for improving the insurability of the complex and for minimizing the cost of property insurance on it. Describe the fire protection factors that the underwriter should consider in making such suggestions.

1-9. An application has been received for commercial property with basic form causes of loss (includes fire, lightning, explosion, vandalism, sprinkler leakage, windstorm, hail, smoke, aircraft, vehicles, riot or civil commotion, sinkhole collapse, and volcanic action) from Music, Inc., an electronics company that produces a well-known line of stereo equipment. All operations are located in a one-story structure that is 25 percent joisted masonry construction and 75 percent masonry noncombustible construction. The risk has three major fire divisions—the warehouse, the manufacturing area, and the office and laboratory. The sprinkler system was installed last year when the building was constructed and covers 75 percent of the total area. In the warehouse, a dry pipe sprinkler system is used; in all other sprinklered locations, a wet pipe sprinkler system is in operation.

The building is protected by guards on duty between 4:30 PM and 7:30 AM. A local burglar alarm system covers all door openings (exterior and interior) of the warehouse portion of the building.

The property is located in an industrial park and is flanked by a four-story, multiple-occupancy manufacturing building and a warehouse. Asphalt parking lots are on the other two sides.

All metal stamping, bending, and forming operations for component casings are carried out in an area cut off from the rest of the plant. The dip tank for painting metal parts is located in the sprinklered portion of the building. The highest concentration of values is in the drying rooms, where dipped items are stored after passing through drying ovens.

Identify and analyze the major construction, occupancy, protection, and exposure hazards of this risk.

Educational Objective 2
Explain how insurable interest, policy provisions for valuing losses, and insurance to value affect a loss payment amount under property insurance.

Key Words and Phrases

Replacement cost

Actual cash value

Coinsurance clause

Review Questions

2-1. What is the source of the most common insurable interest in property?

2-2. What are the most common property valuation methods?

2-3. Identify the insurer benefits associated with encouragement of insurance-to-value provisions.

Educational Objective 3

Explain how underwriters use policy amount, amount subject, normal loss expectancy (NLE), probable maximum loss (PML), and maximum foreseeable loss (MFL) to measure potential loss severity.

Key Word or Phrase

Noncombustible construction

Review Questions

3-1. Explain why policy amount is the least useful figure for determining potential loss severity.

3-2. What expression do underwriters often use to explain the concept of amount subject?

3-3. List the elements used to determine the normal loss expectancy (NLE) for a risk.

3-4. Under what assumption do underwriters often operate when calculating probable maximum loss (PML)?

3-5. Explain the concept of maximum foreseeable loss (MFL) as it applies to fire losses.

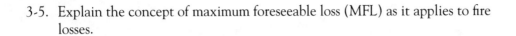

Educational Objective 4

Describe the underwriting considerations for business income and extra expense coverage.

Key Word or Phrase

COPE

Review Questions

4-1. Describe the three steps underwriters can use to estimate probable maximum loss (PML) for business income coverage.

4-2. Provide some examples of factors that could affect the duration of a business interruption.

4-3. What must occur in order for there to be a covered loss of use, loss of business income, or extra expense loss?

4-4. Describe the key elements of a disaster recovery plan.

Educational Objective 5

Describe the underwriting considerations and risk control techniques associated with employee dishonesty and crimes committed by others.

Review Questions

5-1. Identify the conditions that underwriters should ensure exist before issuing employee dishonesty insurance.

5-2. List three examples of controls that can minimize employee dishonest losses.

5-3. Identify six factors underwriters analyzing crimes committed by others loss exposures must consider.

5-4. Why are moral and morale hazards particularly important with regard to crime?

5-5. Identify the two important functions private protection systems serve.

Educational Objective 6
Describe the loss exposures and the underwriting considerations for commercial general liability insurance.

Key Words and Phrases
Vicarious liability

Breach of warranty

Implied warranty of merchantability

Implied warranty of fitness for purpose

Negligence

Strict liability (absolute liability)

Review Questions

6-1. Why is the legal status of persons likely to be on the premises an important consideration when underwriting commercial general liability loss exposures?

6-2. Why do operations-oriented businesses generally have a greater property loss damage exposure than premises-oriented businesses?

6-3. What factors can account for the differences in exposure between two premises?

6-4. What are some of the loss exposures an underwriter would consider for products liability coverage applications?

Educational Objective 7

Describe the underwriting considerations for personal and commercial auto insurance.

Key Words and Phrases

Credit scoring

Class rate

Review Questions

7-1. Why is driving experience important when evaluating a personal auto applicant?

7-2. What information should an underwriter have to analyze a commercial automobile submission?

7-3. What are the characteristics of good fleet safety programs?

Application Question

7-4. An agent for an insurer sends an application for a personal automobile policy to an underwriter. The application contains only the applicant's name, birth date, and marital status, and the year, make, and model of her vehicle.

    a. Identify essential underwriting information that is not given in the application.

    b. How would the essential underwriting information differ if the applicant's vehicle to be insured were a truck used for commercial purposes instead of a personal auto?

Educational Objective 8

Describe the underwriting considerations for workers compensation insurance.

Key Word or Phrase

Experience modification factor

Review Questions

8-1. Give four examples of specific on-premises hazards that could lead to workers compensation losses.

8-2. What three aspects should an underwriter consider when evaluating off-premises hazards?

8-3. Why should a workers compensation underwriter investigate an applicant's use of temporary and seasonal workers?

8-4. Why should a workers compensation underwriter investigate an applicant's use of subcontractors?

8-5. What should underwriters consider when assessing an insured's management?

Educational Objective 9
Describe the underwriting considerations for umbrella and excess liability insurance.

Key Words and Phrases
Umbrella liability insurance

Excess liability insurance

Drop-down coverage

Review Questions

9-1. What three functions are most umbrella policies designed to serve?

9-2. What is the primary underwriting concern associated with umbrella and excess liability policies?

9-3. What elements of underlying insurance coverage can affect the underwriting of umbrella and excess liability policies?

9-4. What is the best method for assessing an insurer's solvency?

Answers to Assignment 5 Questions

NOTE: These answers are provided to give students a basic understanding of acceptable types of responses. They often are not the only valid answers and are not intended to provide an exhaustive response to the questions.

Educational Objective 1

1-1. Fire-resistive construction is designed to withstand damage by fire for at least two hours. Noncombustible construction has exterior walls, roof, and floor constructed of noncombustible materials. A noncombustible building is not as resistant to fire damage as one with fire-resistive construction because its unprotected steel structural supports bend when subjected to the heat of a typical fire.

1-2. The interior finish of a building determines how combustible the structure may be and is an indicator of the fuel load. Buildings with extensive interior features such as draperies, carpeting, and paneling provide fuel for a fire. Furthermore, certain furnishings may be a source of noxious gases and excessive smoke, which pose a life safety concern.

1-3. The age of a building should be considered because of these factors:

- A different building code might have been in effect when the building was constructed. Consequently, the building might lack protective features and systems generally considered essential today.

- Complying with current building codes might increase the cost of making repairs after a loss.

- Heating, cooling, electrical, and fire protection systems might be obsolete.

- The building might have been intended for a different occupancy and might not be suitable for its current use.

- Conversion and remodeling might have created concealed spaces in which fire could burn undetected and spread rapidly.

- Alterations and repairs made over the years might have left unprotected openings in vertical and horizontal firestops.

- The building's condition might have deteriorated for numerous reasons, including normal wear and tear, hard use, or lack of maintenance.

- The value of an older building might be difficult to determine, especially if the builder used construction techniques and materials that are no longer available.

1-4. Most firefighting services are not capable of fighting a fire from the exterior of high-rises because of ladder capacity. Therefore, firefighters must enter the structure and fight the fire from inside. High-rise structures also generally have a large number of occupants. Life safety is always the first priority for firefighters, and extinguishing the blaze is second.

1-5. Principal ignition sources include these:

- Friendly fires that escape containment

- Friction that generates enough heat to ignite nearby combustible material

- Electricity that produces sparks or heat that can ignite exposed combustibles

- Chemical reactions that produce heat sufficient to cause ignition

1-6. The factors are related to fire protection equipment and services. These include the adequacy of the equipment available, the water supply, and the response time.

1-7. External exposures are by definition outside the insured's control. Often, little can be done from a risk control standpoint to reduce external exposures. However, fire walls, fire doors, special barriers, and parapets can reduce the probability that an external fire will spread to the insured property. Clear space between buildings, good water supply, quick response from the fire department, and internal and external automatic sprinkler systems are additional methods of controlling external loss exposures.

1-8. The protection factors include public and private protection considerations. Public protection depends on services provided by local authorities. In rural areas such as this, less public protection may be available, or the proposed shopping center may be located a great distance from the fire department and/or fire hydrants. Such a situation would also result in a higher property rate because the slower response time may result in a greater degree of damage from fire or other perils. Private protection measures, which include partial sprinkler protection, overnight guard service, and a local fire alarm, generally result in a reduced property premium.

1-9. Construction: Construction appears to be acceptable. Masonry noncombustible will sustain less fire damage than the joisted masonry areas. It is important to determine which operations are being conducted in the 25 percent of the building that is joisted masonry construction. Fire divisions will assist in limiting the horizontal spread of fire from one section of the building to another.

Occupancy: The areas of greatest concern are the exposures and hazards related to the manufacturing operations. Potential hazards include heat treatment, electrical and wiring systems, and drying ovens.

Improper storage of flammables or other hazardous materials may increase the likelihood of a property loss. Housekeeping and maintenance are also important considerations. The contents of this occupancy would include finished stereo equipment, unfinished components, and work in progress. These would all be highly damageable from either fire or accidental sprinkler leakage.

Protection: No information is provided regarding public protection. The underwriter would need to determine the public protection class, the availability of fire department service, and proximity to fire hydrants.

Private protection is adequate and includes partial sprinkler protection, overnight guard service, and a local alarm.

Exposure: The property is located in an industrial park with similar-type occupancies as exposing properties. The immediate exposing structure is the adjacent four-story manufacturing and warehouse building. Of concern would be any hazardous manufacturing occupancies in surrounding buildings. The asphalt parking lots are a positive factor and provide clear space, which reduces the possibility of damage to the covered building as the result of a loss at an exposing structure.

Educational Objective 2

2-1. The most common insurable interest in property comes from outright ownership.

2-2. The most common property valuation methods are replacement cost and actual cash value.

2-3. The insurer benefits when underwriters encourage insurance to value because these results are then promoted:

- Higher limits of property

- An adequately insured book of business

- Competitive status

Educational Objective 3

3-1. The amount of insurance is the least useful figure for determining potential loss severity because the amount of insurance purchased could have little bearing on the amount of the loss.

3-2. Underwriters often use the expression "within four walls" to explain the concept of amount subject.

3-3. In determining the NLE for a risk, these elements are used for consideration:

- Construction

- Protection (positive pressure ventilation/sprinklers)

- Business interruption contingency plans

- Fire divisions

- Susceptibility of contents to damage and combustibility

- Operational hazards

3-4. Underwriters often calculate PML based on the assumption that anything that can go wrong will go wrong.

3-5. MFL is an estimate of the financial cost of the loss that would occur if all protection measures (automatic and manual) were to fail and no effective fire department response occurred.

Educational Objective 4

4-1. Underwriters can estimate the PML for business income coverage in three steps:

- Determine the most serious direct loss that is likely to occur.

- Calculate the longest period of restoration that this loss can reasonably be expected to cause.

- Compute the largest loss of business income that the insured is likely to sustain during a period of this length.

4-2. Examples of factors that could affect the duration of a business interruption include these:

- Time required to rebuild the insured premises

- Seasonality of the business

- Bottlenecks

- Computer systems

- Long production processes

- Availability of substitutes

- Business continuity and disaster recovery planning

4-3. A covered loss of use, loss of business income, or extra expense loss cannot occur without direct damage to property at the insured premises.

4-4. A disaster recovery plan should include detailed written plans to restore the production process if part or all of the facility and equipment were destroyed. It should indicate what would be necessary if each part of the process were destroyed. The plan could also indicate whether continuation of the operation is feasible following certain types of damage.

Educational Objective 5

5-1. Before issuing a policy, underwriters should be satisfied that these conditions exist:

- There is no evidence of a moral hazard. (If there is, other coverages probably should not be written either.)

- Burglary and robbery risk control systems should be in place and maintained. Defenses against external crime also deter employee crime.

- As with other coverages, amounts of insurance should fall within the limits prescribed by the insurer's underwriting guidelines.

- The organization should be managed soundly. Management controls provide evidence of management's care and concern.

5-2. Any three of these examples are controls that can minimize employee dishonesty losses:

- New hires are screened for prior criminal activity, and their references are checked.

- Seasoned employees are evaluated before they are promoted, especially for moves into sensitive positions.

- A substance-abuse screening program is in place. Underwriters regard this as a positive sign because substance dependency creates potential for employee dishonesty.

- The rate and level of employee turnover is appropriate given the insured's business (employee turnover can increase the insured's loss exposure).

- Termination procedures are well defined. The computer passwords of employees who had worked in sensitive areas are revoked, and keys or access cards are returned upon termination.

- Management is sensitive to dramatic changes in employee behavior, such as sudden or drastic lifestyle changes, which might indicate employee dishonesty.

- Periodic audits are conducted to evaluate accounts receivable, cash accounts, inventories, and disbursements.

- Bank reconciliations are done to ensure that company records and bank records agree.

- Employees monitor one another through a division of authority among employees.

- Annual vacations of a minimum length of time are required. This acts as a control because some embezzlement methods require a daily adjustment of records.

- Duties are rotated, a practice that helps to uncover irregularities or embezzlement.

- Two-person or dual control systems are in place on some items, such as the vault, cash, and other items susceptible to theft.

5-3. Underwriters analyzing crimes committed by others loss exposures consider six factors:

- Susceptibility and marketability

- Property location

- Nature of the occupancy

- Moral and morale hazards

- Public protection

- Coverage and price modifications

5-4. Moral hazards and morale hazards are particularly important with regard to crime because a dishonest insured can readily dispose of inventory and arrange a fraudulent claim. Likewise, a lax attitude toward loss might mean that precautions and protective measures are not consistently adhered to, thereby creating an environment in which a loss is more likely to occur.

5-5. Private protection systems generally serve two important functions: to prevent crime losses and to reduce losses that do occur.

Educational Objective 6

6-1. The legal status of persons likely to be on the premises determines the policyholder's legal duty to these persons and the expected standard of care.

6-2. Operations exposures involve substantial work on the premises of others. The work of trade contractors and other construction-related work exposes the property of others to damage. The possible use of heavy equipment increases the potential for serious property damage. The major sources of property damage losses are fire, collapse, water damage, and, in some cases, pollution.

6-3. The differences in exposure between two premises may be a result of location, type of business, or time in business, or a combination of the three.

6-4. When reviewing applications for products liability coverage, an underwriter would consider the inherent hazards of the product, the types of representations or promises about the product made to consumers in sales materials and advertising, and whether the product's technical manuals accurately reflect safety precautions required in its assembly or repair. The underwriter would also consider if the product's packaging adequately protects the product so that it will operate properly when used and who the ultimate consumer for the product is.

Educational Objective 7

7-1. Driving experience is a crucial component of an underwriter's review of a driver, because driving experience is a likely indicator of a driver's future actions and the chance of loss. Underwriters evaluate a driver's prior accidents and prior moving violations. The driver's prior loss history may indicate poor driving habits, recklessness, or simply a lack of skill.

7-2. Factors relating to both the driver and the vehicle are considered. In addition to information about the driver, underwriters consider the weight and type of vehicle, use of vehicle, radius of vehicle operation, and special industry classifications.

7-3. Good fleet safety programs are clear, concise, and written at a level appropriate for the program user. They should contain practical procedures that employees can follow and the account's management can support.

7-4.

    a. Essential underwriting information that is not given in the application includes these elements:

- Use of the vehicle
- Driving record
- Territory
- Occupation
- Personal characteristics
- Physical condition of driver
- Safety equipment

b. The essential information for a commercial vehicle would also include the use of the vehicle, the radius of operation, and the applicability of any special industry classifications.

Educational Objective 8

8-1. Four examples of specific on-premises hazards that could lead to workers compensation losses are housekeeping, maintenance, occupational disease, and hazards leading to cumulative trauma injuries.

8-2. Three aspects should be considered when evaluating off-premises hazards: (1) the duration of travel, (2) the mode of transportation, and (3) the hazards at remote job sites.

8-3. A workers compensation underwriter should investigate an applicant's use of temporary and seasonal workers because temporary or seasonal workers may lack sufficient training, which increases the risk of injury. These workers also present a potential moral hazard because they could fake an injury while on the job and receive workers compensation benefits.

8-4. Most workers compensation laws hold contractors responsible for workers' compensation benefits to employees of its uninsured subcontractors. The underwriter needs to determine whether adequate insurance is in place and, if not, to charge the appropriate rate.

8-5. In evaluating management of an insured, the underwriter should consider the willingness and ability of management to minimize hazards and reduce losses. When assessing management, underwriters also should perform a wage analysis and consider whether management provides healthcare benefits for its employees.

Educational Objective 9

9-1. Most umbrella policies are designed to serve three functions:

- Provide excess liability limits above all specified underlying policies
- Provide coverage when the aggregate limits of the underlying policies have been exhausted
- Provide coverage for gaps in the underlying policies

9-2. For umbrella and excess liability policies, loss severity, as opposed to loss frequency, is the primary underwriting concern.

9-3. These elements of the underlying insurance can affect underwriting:

- Type of insurance
- Name of insurer
- Applicable limits and deductibles
- Premium for bodily injury liability coverages
- Premium for property damage liability coverages
- Details of extensions of coverage beyond standard policy provisions

9-4. An insurer's solvency may be assessed based on the rating it receives from a recognized service such as A.M. Best or Standard & Poor's.

Direct Your Learning

Risk Control and Premium Auditing

Educational Objectives

After learning the content of this assignment, you should be able to:

1. Describe the goals of insurer risk control activities.
2. Describe the risk control services provided by insurers.
3. Explain how risk control cooperates with other insurer functions.
4. Explain why premium audits are conducted.
5. Describe the premium auditing process.
6. Explain why premium audits must be accurate.
7. Explain how premium auditing contributes to other insurer functions.

Outline

▶ **Insurer Risk Control Goals**
   A. Earn a Profit
   B. Meet Customer Needs
   C. Comply With Legal Requirements
   D. Fulfill Duty to Society

▶ **Risk Control Services Provided by Insurers**
   A. Conducting Physical Surveys
   B. Performing Risk Analysis and Improvement
   C. Developing Safety Management Programs
   D. Factors Affecting Service Levels
      1. Line of Insurance
      2. Commercial Insured Size
      3. Types of Loss Exposures Insured
      4. Potential Legal Liability

▶ **Cooperation Between Risk Control and Other Insurer Functions**
   A. Underwriting
   B. Marketing and Sales
   C. Premium Auditing
   D. Claims
   E. Producers

▶ **Reasons for Premium Auditing**
   A. Determine Correct Premiums
   B. Collect Ratemaking Data
   C. Meet Regulatory Requirements
   D. Deter and Detect Fraud
   E. Reinforce Confidence of Insureds
   F. Obtain Additional Information

▶ **Premium Auditing Process**
   A. Planning
   B. Reviewing Operations
   C. Determining Employment Relationships
   D. Finding and Evaluating Books or Records
   E. Auditing the Books and Records
   F. Analyzing and Verifying Premium-Related Data
   G. Reporting the Findings

▶ **Importance of Accurate Premium Audits**
   A. Importance for the Insured
   B. Importance for the Insurer
      1. Financial Position
      2. Customer Retention
      3. Goodwill
      4. Efficiency
      5. Collections
   C. Importance for Insurance Rates

▶ **Premium Auditing Contributions**
   A. Underwriting
   B. Marketing and Sales
   C. Claims
   D. Risk Control

Plan to register with The Institutes well in advance of your exam. For complete information regarding exam dates and fees, please visit our Web page, www.TheInstitutes.org/forms, where you can access and print exam registration information.

For each assignment, you should define or describe each of the Key Words and Phrases and answer each of the Review and Application Questions.

Educational Objective 1
Describe the goals of insurer risk control activities.

Review Questions

1-1. Describe how an insurer's risk control activities can assist in meeting the insurer's profit goals.

1-2. Describe the benefits an insurer receives by offering risk control services through agents in the independent agency system.

Educational Objective 2
Describe the risk control services provided by insurers.

Key Words and Phrases
Moral hazard

Morale hazard (attitudinal hazard)

Review Questions

2-1. Describe the three categories of insurer risk control activities.

2-2. What factors affect the level of risk control service that insurers provide, and the insureds to whom it is provided?

Educational Objective 3
Explain how risk control cooperates with other insurer functions.

Review Questions

3-1. Explain how the risk control function provides information to underwriters that enables them to make better underwriting decisions.

3-2. Compare how the risk control function assists an insurer's marketing staff with applicants and with existing customers.

3-3. How can risk control's visit to an insured at the beginning of a policy period assist a premium auditor?

Educational Objective 4
Explain why premium audits are conducted.

Key Words and Phrases

Premium audit

Exposure unit (unit of exposure)

Loss costs

Review Questions

4-1. Explain the primary reason for premium auditing.

4-2. Describe how premium auditing contributes data to the ratemaking process.

4-3. How does premium auditing reinforce the confidence of insureds?

Educational Objective 5
Describe the premium auditing process.

Key Words and Phrases

Test Audit

Premium pay (shift differential)

Deposit premium

Review Questions

5-1. Describe the factors premium auditors consider as they decide whether to conduct a field audit.

5-2. Describe the process of auditing the risk.

5-3. Explain the importance of the premium auditor's determination of employment relationships.

Application Question

5-4. A premium auditor has been assigned to audit ABC, a small department store, for Danforth Insurance Co. Danforth insures ABC for workers compensation and general liability. The workers compensation premium is based on payroll, and the liability premium is based on sales. Describe the process a premium auditor might use in auditing ABC's accounting records.

Educational Objective 6
Explain why premium audits must be accurate.

Key Word or Phrase

Experience modification

Review Questions

6-1. Explain why accurate premium audits are important for insureds.

6-2. Describe three ways that the accuracy of premium audits affect an insurer's financial position.

6-3. How does the accuracy of a premium audit affect an insurer's collection of premium?

Application Question

6-4. The premium auditors for Danforth Insurance Co., an insurer operating in the western part of a state, consider a commercial industry exposure to be Classification X. The premium auditors for Forthley Insurance Co., an insurer operating in the eastern part of the state, consider the same commercial industry exposure to be Classification Y. Explain how these different classifications affect insurance rates in the state.

Educational Objective 7

Explain how premium auditing contributes to other insurer functions.

Review Questions

7-1. Describe premium auditing's contribution to underwriting.

    a. Explain the importance of premium auditing in classifying insured exposures.

    b. Explain the importance of premium auditing in the identification of inadequate exposure estimates.

c. Explain the importance of premium auditing in providing information on the desirability of an account.

7-2. Explain why timely premium audits are important to marketing and sales.

7-3. Explain the importance of premium auditing's verification of classification codes.

Answers to Assignment 6 Questions

NOTE: These answers are provided to give students a basic understanding of acceptable types of responses. They often are not the only valid answers and are not intended to provide an exhaustive response to the questions.

Educational Objective 1

1-1. Risk control activities can assist insurers in reaching their profit objectives by improving underwriting decisions; increasing premium volume by making marginal accounts acceptable and winning new business; encouraging insureds to improve risk control; and reducing insureds' losses. Risk control may be an additional revenue source for insurers that sell "unbundled" loss control services and assist in reducing errors and omissions claims against the insurer.

1-2. By providing risk control services through agents in the independent agency system, an insurer may enhance its relationship with the producers, staff, and customers of the independent agency; increase its own market share as well as that of the agency; attract and retain higher-quality accounts; and help the agency and its customers accomplish their goals.

Educational Objective 2

2-1. Conducting physical surveys—Inspections of the customer's premises take place, including interviews with management and employees, to evaluate physical hazards affecting the customer's exposures based on the coverages provided and management's ability to control exposures effectively.

Performing risk analysis and improvement—In addition to inspecting the premises and providing a physical survey report, the risk control department can analyze the customer's loss history. Based on this review, formal written recommendations on reducing hazards are submitted to the insured. Risk control personnel may also provide training, information, or counseling services, such as safety programs or fire protection systems testing.

Developing safety management programs—This activity involves a complete evaluation of the insured's operations. The evaluation is reviewed with the insured, and the risk control consultants then work with the insured to establish risk control objectives, select appropriate risk control measures, and establish procedures to monitor the program.

2-2. Several factors affect the level of risk control service provided and the insureds to whom it is provided. One factor is the line of insurance. An insurer is unlikely to provide extensive risk control services in personal lines. Insurers usually provide risk control services to commercial insureds. The size of the commercial account will often determine the level and extent of risk control services provided. Another factor is the type of loss exposures covered. Usually, large and complex industrial exposures will receive the most sophisticated level of risk control services. Finally, potential legal liability and state laws can influence insurers in decisions regarding risk control services.

Educational Objective 3

3-1. The information that the risk control function provides to underwriters consists primarily of field inspection reports on the premises and operations of new applicants and of existing insureds who are renewing their policies. These inspection reports provide a clear profile of the applicant's loss exposures and related hazards. Additionally, risk control representatives can provide technical information, such as fire hazards associated with new building materials, health hazards of materials or production processes, and new techniques or equipment for materials handling.

3-2. The risk control function can help make an applicant acceptable by providing assistance with reducing loss exposures and thus help marketing reach sales goals. Also, risk control can identify opportunities for additional coverage that can be provided to applicants after a review of their premises. Risk control assists marketing with existing customers through regular, courteous service and assistance in improving safety and protecting their interests.

3-3. Premium auditors usually visit insureds at the end of a policy period, and this is often after the point at which recordkeeping deficiencies resulting from an insured's lack of knowledge or misunderstanding can be corrected. Risk control representatives can use the opportunity of their inspection early in the policy period to help improve documentation.

Educational Objective 4

4-1. The primary reason for premium auditing is to determine the correct premium for the policy period. For many commercial insurance policies, the premium paid at the beginning of the policy period is a provisional premium based on an estimate of the extent of operations to be insured. The actual premium can be calculated only after the end of the policy period, when the exact exposure units or premium bases during the policy period are known. Premium auditing determines those exposure units and premium bases at the end of the policy period.

4-2. Calculating actuarially credible rates begins with data about claim payments, earned premiums, and insured exposure units for each rating classification. Although claim reports provide the necessary information on claims for a given period, the premium volume and total insured loss exposures by class cannot be determined with any degree of certainty without compiling data from premium audits.

4-3. Competent premium audits can contribute to insureds' confidence that they are receiving fair treatment from their insurer. Those who observe the audit process realize that insureds are treated according to uniform and equitable standards. A good premium auditor also explains the audit procedure and creates a favorable impression of the insurer.

Educational Objective 5

5-1. The decision about whether to conduct a field audit is influenced by legal requirements, premium size, the insured's operations, prior audit experience, nature of the policy, cost of auditing, geographical factors, and staffing requirements. Some field audits are mandatory, such as workers compensation audits in some states. Advisory organization rules usually require audits of all policies involving a premium above a certain amount and may restrict audit waivers. Predictive modeling may be used in the planning process to guide decisions on when to conduct field audits.

5-2. Auditing the risk is a process premium auditors use to review the operations, organization, and business practices of the insured. This process seeks to identify new loss exposures. Additionally, this process assesses management quality and cooperation, previously unreported risk classifications, and unusual hazards.

5-3. Premium auditors must determine those employees covered by the types of insurance for which premiums are based on payroll. Employees' payroll might constitute the premium base for both workers compensation and general liability policies, but the definition of "employee" is not necessarily the same for both coverages.

5-4. A premium auditor would likely verify premium-related data against the general accounting records of ABC to reconcile any discrepancies. For the workers compensation premium, the auditor would examine the payroll records to determine the job and wages for each employee to be certain that employees are classified in the correct job classification and their earnings correctly reported. For the general liability premium, the premium auditor would compare sales figures from the accounting records with the premium data to determine if there has been any significant increase or decrease in sales that would result in a premium adjustment.

Educational Objective 6

6-1. If there are premium audit errors, an insured could be charged an incorrect premium. Some insureds may be charged more than their proportional share, resulting in a negative financial impact and a potential for a competitive disadvantage. Other insureds may be charged less than their proportional share, resulting in an undeserved financial windfall and a potential for an undeserved competitive advantage.

Additionally, inaccurate premium audits can result in an incorrect experience modification calculation, resulting in future incorrect premiums.

6-2. The accuracy of premium audits affects an insurer's financial position in three ways.

   a. Accurate classification of loss exposures is important to ensure equitable and accurate insurance rates.

   b. Timely premium audits directly affect an insurer's cash flow management. Delays in audits can have a negative affect on an insurer's cash flow. It is also important that the deposit premium charged to renewal accounts is correct and based on an accurate premium audit.

   c. Premium that has been developed by premium audit is fully earned and, consequently, has an immediate effect on an insurer's policyholder surplus, which determines the amount of new business an insurer can write. It is important that the premium developed by premium audit be accurate and, thus, be accurately reflected in the insurer's surplus.

6-3. Insureds are less likely to pay premium bills that they believe are incorrect. An insured's challenge of a bill can result in a re-audit and significant effort and delay for the insurer's collection department before the bill is paid.

6-4. The inconsistency distorts the resulting loss data from both classes and leads to inequitable rates for all insureds in the state for those two classes.

Educational Objective 7

7-1. Premium auditing contributes significant information in many areas to underwriting. Effective cooperation between underwriters and premium auditors is essential to ensuring that existing accounts remain profitable.

    a. Although underwriting must establish the classifications when the policy is issued, the information submitted is occasionally incomplete or inaccurate. Properly classifying an account can be complex, and the operations of insureds can change. The premium audit, conducted at the end of the policy period, can reveal any classification changes necessary to update the policy. Premium auditors notify underwriting of any discrepancies between the classifications on the policy and those classifications that are proper for the operation.

    b. An important contribution of the premium auditing function to underwriting is the identification of inadequate exposure estimates. When the insured exposure has been underestimated or incorrectly classified, an inadequate deposit premium for a renewal will result. Additionally, premium auditors can identify new exposures for which underwriting information might be deficient.

    c. Premium auditors are in a position to provide underwriting with information on the desirability of an account. Premium auditors visit the insured's premises, meet with management, review business records, and observe the employees and operations. A premium auditor can thus become aware of physical, moral, and morale hazards that might indicate that an account is undesirable.

7-2. The premium audit may result in a refund of premium owed to the insured. A delay in a refund of premium could adversely affect the insurer's future marketing efforts to that insured. Therefore, it is important for the premium audit to be completed timely to identify any refund due to the insured.

7-3. A premium auditor verifying or correcting the classification codes assigned to an insured's claims provides a contribution to the insurer's claim function. This also provides an important contribution to insurance regulators. By ensuring that claims and premiums are matched in the same classifications, the credibility of rates is improved.

Direct Your Learning

Overview of the Claim Function

Educational Objectives

After learning the content of this assignment, you should be able to:

1. Identify the goals of the claim function, the users of claim information, and the parties with whom claim personnel interact.

2. Describe the claim department structure, types and functions of claim personnel, and claim personnel performance measures.

3. Describe the following activities in the claim handling process:

   - Acknowledging and assigning the claim

   - Identifying the policy and setting reserves

   - Contacting the insured or the insured's representative

   - Investigating the claim

   - Documenting the claim

   - Determining the cause of loss, liability, and the loss amount

   - Concluding the claim

4. Explain how the law of bad faith relates to an insurer's duty of good faith and fair dealing and how the legal environment affects the law of bad faith.

5. Describe the elements of good-faith claim handling.

Outline

▶ **The Claim Function**

A. Claim Function Goals

   1. Complying With the Contractual Promise

   2. Supporting the Insurer's Financial Goals

B. Claim Information Users

   1. Marketing

   2. Underwriting

   3. Actuarial

C. Claim Department Contacts

   1. The Public

   2. Lawyers

   3. State Regulators

▶ **Claim Department**

A. Claim Department Structure

B. Claim Personnel

   1. Staff Claim Representatives

   2. Independent Adjusters

   3. Third-Party Administrators

   4. Producers

   5. Public Adjusters

C. Claim Performance Measures

   1. Profitability Measures

   2. Quality Measures

▶ **Claim Handling Process**

A. Acknowledging and Assigning the Claim

B. Identifying the Policy and Setting Reserves

   1. Identifying the Policy

   2. Setting Reserves

   3. Causes of Reserve Errors

C. Contacting the Insured or the Insured's Representative

   1. Good Faith

   2. Waiver and Estoppel

D. Investigating the Claim

   1. Claim Investigations

   2. Subrogation Investigation and Recovery

E. Documenting the Claim

   1. Diary Systems

   2. File Status Notes

   3. File Reports

F. Determining the Cause of Loss, Liability, and the Loss Amount

G. Concluding the Claim

   1. Payments

   2. Claim Denial

   3. Alternative Dispute Resolution

   4. Litigation

   5. Closing Reports

▶ **Law of Bad Faith**

A. Development of the Law of Bad Faith

B. Duty of Good Faith and Fair Dealing

   1. Public Interest

   2. Higher Standard of Conduct

C. Legal Environment of Bad Faith

▶ **Elements of Good-Faith Claim Handling**

A. Thorough, Timely, and Unbiased Investigation

   1. Thorough Investigation

   2. Timely Investigation

   3. Unbiased Investigation

   4. Federal Statute

   5. Health Insurance Portability and Accountability Act of 1996

   6. Gramm-Leach-Bliley Act

   7. Sarbanes-Oxley Act

   8. Fair Credit Reporting Act

B. Complete and Accurate Documentation

C. Fair Evaluation

D. Good-Faith Negotiation

E. Regular and Prompt Communication

F. Competent Legal Advice

G. Effective Claim Management

   1. Consistent Supervision

   2. Thorough Training

   3. Manageable Caseloads

Set aside a specific, realistic amount of time to study every day.

For each assignment, you should define or describe each of the Key Words and Phrases and answer each of the Review and Application Questions.

Educational Objective 1

Identify the goals of the claim function, the users of claim information, and the parties with whom claim personnel interact.

Review Questions

1-1.   Describe the primary goals of the claim function.

1-2.   Differentiate between a first-party claim and a third-party claim.

1-3.   Describe how claim managers can help maintain an insurer's underwriting profit.

1-4. Describe the marketing department's need for claim information.

1-5. What actions might an underwriter take on an account when a claim representative reports either negative or positive loss exposure characteristics found during claim investigations of homes and work sites?

1-6. What is the result for actuaries (and insurers) when claim payments are recorded accurately and realistic reserves are set in the insurer's claim processing system?

1-7. Explain how a claim representative's contact with an insured or a claimant after a loss is crucial to the insurer's public image.

1-8. Describe claim representatives' interactions with lawyers.

1-9. Identify three circumstances under which claim representatives interact with state insurance regulators.

Application Question

1-10. An insurer's management is concerned with garnering the goodwill of the public. Explain how the insurer's claim department management could devise a philosophy that would address management's concerns and meet the insurer's claim function goals.

Educational Objective 2

Describe the claim department structure, types and functions of claim personnel, and claim personnel performance measures.

Key Words and Phrases

Third-party administrator (TPA)

Independent adjuster

Loss ratio

Incurred losses

Earned premiums

Expense ratio

Review Questions

2-1. Describe or diagram the claim department structure in which you work or with which you are most familiar

2-2. Describe each of the following claim personnel to distinguish each position from the others.

   a.   Staff claim representatives

b. Independent adjusters

c. Third-party administrators

d. Producers

e. Public adjusters

2-3. Identify the two types of performance measures used to measure claim personnel performance, and list examples of each.

Educational Objective 3

Describe the following activities in the claim handling process:

- **Acknowledging and assigning the claim**
- **Identifying the policy and setting reserves**
- **Contacting the insured or the insured's representative**
- **Investigating the claim**
- **Documenting the claim**
- **Determining the cause of loss, liability, and the loss amount**
- **Concluding the claim**

Key Words and Phrases

Nonwaiver agreement

Reservation of rights letter

Individual case method

Roundtable method

Average value method

Formula method

Expert system method

Loss ratio method

Stairstepping

Subrogation

Mediation

Arbitration

Mini-trial

Summary jury trial

Review Questions

3-1. Regardless of what method is used to assign a claim to a claim representative, what is the goal of assigning the claim?

3-2. When reviewing coverages, if it is apparent from the loss notice that coverage may not be available for the loss, the claim representative should prepare either one of which two documents to notify the insured of this concern while still preserving the insurer's rights?

3-3. What are two reserving methods that may result in a more realistic reserve and may be used to avoid the problem of stairstepping reserves?

3-4. After verifying coverage and setting reserves, what preparations should the claim representative make before making the initial contact with any of the parties to a claim?

3-5. What two determinations does the claim representative make based on the facts of the case?

3-6. What checks must a claim representative perform to ensure that the proper parties are paid when preparing to make a loss payment?

Educational Objective 4

Explain how the law of bad faith relates to an insurer's duty of good faith and fair dealing and how the legal environment affects the law of bad faith.

Key Word or Phrase

Breach of contract

Review Questions

4-1. Explain why the law of bad faith developed.

4-2. Describe the two attributes of the insurance contract that contributed to the development of bad-faith claims.

4-3. Explain why claim representatives must stay informed about the bases of bad-faith claims in the states in which they handle claims.

Educational Objective 5
Describe the elements of good-faith claim handling.

Review Questions

5-1. Identify the elements of good-faith claim handling.

5-2. Investigations that are thorough, timely, and unbiased are the foundation of good-faith claim handling. Explain how claim representatives should use these standards when conducting investigations.

a.   Thorough

b. Timely

c. Unbiased

5-3. Explain why claim representatives should be aware of these federal statutes, designed to ensure privacy of confidential information:

a. Health Insurance Portability and Accountability Act of 1996 (HIPAA)

b. Gramm-Leach-Bliley Act (GLB)

c. Sarbanes-Oxley Act

d. Fair Credit Reporting Act

5-4. Explain why it is important for a claim file to provide a complete and accurate account of all the activities and actions taken by the claim representative.

5-5. Identify the sources that claim representatives can use to assist them in making a knowledgeable claim evaluation.

5-6. Contrast the standards for claim representatives and lawyers in good-faith negotiations.

5-7. Describe the important results that are achieved through regular and prompt communication with the insured.

5-8. Identify the three critical elements of good-faith claim handling.

Answers to Assignment 7 Questions

NOTE: These answers are provided to give students a basic understanding of acceptable types of responses. They often are not the only valid answers and are not intended to provide an exhaustive response to the questions.

Educational Objective 1

1-1. The primary goals of the claim function are complying with the contractual promise to pay losses that are covered by the policy and supporting the insurer's financial goals.

1-2. First-party claims are made by the insured directly against the insurer. Third-party claims are made indirectly by someone against the insured to whom the insured might be liable.

1-3. Claim managers can help maintain an insurer's underwriting profit by managing all claim function expenses, setting appropriate spending policies, and using appropriately priced providers and services.

1-4. The marketing department needs information about customer satisfaction, timeliness of settlements, and other variables that assist in marketing the insurance product.

1-5. The underwriter may adjust the premium or take other actions to accommodate the difference in the exposure in response to loss exposure characteristics found during claim investigations.

1-6. When claim payments are recorded accurately and realistic reserves are set in the insurer's claim processing system, the raw data that actuaries use to develop rates will be accurate, and the rates will reflect the insurer's loss experience.

1-7. The claim representative is an insured's and a claimant's primary contact with the insurer; therefore, claim service significantly affects an insured's or a claimant's satisfaction with an insurer. The claim representative's skill at communicating directly with claimants influences their satisfaction with the insurer. Consequently, the insurer's public image is determined largely by the claim department's behavior.

1-8. Even when litigation against an insured ensues, claim representatives should continue to interact in a cordial, professional manner with claimants' lawyers. When an insurer needs a lawyer either to defend the insured or to defend itself, it will typically hire a lawyer from the jurisdiction in which the claim is submitted. The lawyer will provide advice regarding specific losses and legal issues. Claim representatives will assist the insurer's lawyers as needed by sharing claim details and assembling information that supports the insurer's legal position.

1-9. Three circumstances under which claim representatives interact with state insurance regulators result from insurers' activities in the claim handling process and enforcement of the Unfair Claims Settlement Practices Act or similar legislation. Claim representatives interact with them when regulators license claim representatives, investigate consumer complaints, and perform market conduct investigations.

1-10. The proposed philosophy should emphasize providing insureds with fair, prompt, and equitable service, either directly or indirectly through third-party claim handling. A claim representative should handle a claim in a way that treats all parties involved fairly and equitably and do so in a timely manner. The idea of providing a fair settlement involves paying neither too much nor too little on claims. Combined with the claim department's controlling expenses, this will allow the insurer to achieve profit goals while complying with the contractual promise to pay losses that occur and while building goodwill with customers and the public.

Educational Objective 2

2-1. Answers will vary.

2-2. Claim personnel can be distinguished among one another in these ways:

   a. Staff claim representatives are employees of an insurer, and they handle most claims. They may include inside claim representatives, who handle claims exclusively from inside an insurer's office, and field claim representatives, who handle claims both inside and outside the office.

   b. Independent adjusters are claim representatives with whom insurers contract to handle claims in strategic locations, such as in disaster sites; to meet desired service levels; or when special skills are needed.

   c. Self-insured businesses can often contract with third-party administrators (TPAs) who handle claims, keep claim records, and perform statistical analyses. TPAs are often associated with large independent adjusting firms or with subsidiaries of insurance companies.

   d. Producers can include agents, brokers, employees of insurers, or intermediaries. Insurers give some producers the authority to pay claims up to a certain amount, such as $2,500. Those producers can issue claim payments, called drafts, directly to insureds for covered claims, thus reducing the time an insured waits for payment.

   e. A public adjuster is an organization or a person hired by an insured to represent the insured in a claim in exchange for a fee. Generally, the public adjuster prepares the insured's claim and negotiates the settlement with the staff claim representative or independent adjuster.

2-3. The two types of performance measures and examples are these:

   a. Profitability measures—examples: loss ratio, expense ratio, or combined ratio (trade-basis)

   b. Quality measures—examples: best practices, claim audits, or customer satisfaction

Educational Objective 3

3-1. The goal is to assign the claim to a claim representative who possesses the appropriate skills to handle it.

3-2. The two documents that preserve the insurer's rights when coverage is doubtful are a nonwaiver agreement and a reservation of rights letter. The claim representative should prepare either one of the two documents in such a situation.

3-3. Two reserving methods that are more accurate and that may help avoid stairstepping are the roundtable method and the expert system method.

3-4. Before making contact with any parties to the claim, the claim representative should prepare a list of questions for the insured or claimant and should prepare a set of instructions on how the claim will be handled and what actions the insured or claimant will have to complete as part of the claim process.

3-5. The claim representative determines the cause of the loss and the liability for the loss based on the facts of the case.

3-6. The claim representative must check several sources to ensure the proper parties are paid in a claim payment. These sources include the policy (for additional loss payees or mortgagees), claim documentation for any attorneys or lienholders (such as medical service providers) who should be named as an additional payees, the federal Office of Foreign Asset Control master list of potential terrorists and drug traffickers, and state child support or other judgment databases for outstanding obligations that may require payment first.

Educational Objective 4

4-1. The law of bad faith developed in response to the perception that insurers were placing their own interests ahead of their insureds' interests. In some cases, insureds became personally liable for losses or damages they believed were covered by their insurance, and they sued their insurers for breach of contract. However, in some of these cases, breach of contract remedies were perceived to be inadequate. Eventually, some courts decided that insurers have an implied duty of good faith and fair dealing when settling claims, requiring insurers to value their insureds' interests at least as much as their own. This duty applies by extension to claim representatives. Insurers' failure to comply with this duty can result in a bad-faith claim.

4-2. The two attributes are that insurance contracts involve the public interest and that they require a higher standard of conduct because of the unequal bargaining power of parties. State insurance regulators and courts wish to protect the public interest against illegal business practices and ensure that insurers pay claims that they owe. Because insurers control how claims are resolved, courts have held insurers to a higher standard of conduct to discourage insurers from abusing their position of power.

4-3. Claim representatives must stay informed because the bases on which bad-faith claims can be brought are constantly changing. Court decisions and legislative changes occur frequently. If claim representatives do not stay informed, they put their employer at increased risk of bad-faith claims.

Educational Objective 5

5-1. These are the elements of good-faith claim handling:

- Thorough, timely, and unbiased investigation
- Complete and accurate documentation
- Fair evaluation
- Good-faith negotiation
- Regular and prompt communication
- Competent legal advice
- Effective claim management

5-2. A claim representative uses these standards as the foundation of good-faith claim handling:

a. Claim representatives should thoroughly investigate claims and collect all relevant and necessary evidence. Investigation should continue as long as new facts develop or become available. Claim representatives should develop the information and documentation necessary to determine liability and damages and should make decisions once they believe they have sufficient information to do so.

b. An insured who makes a claim expects prompt contact from the claim representative. Most insurers have guidelines requiring the claim representative to contact the insured and the claimant within a specific period, such as twenty-four hours after the claim has been submitted. Documentation of timely contact in the claim file can help prove an insurer's use of good-faith claim handling procedures and/or the insurer's compliance with the provisions of the Model Act.

c. Claim representatives should pursue all relevant evidence, especially evidence that establishes the claim's legitimacy, without bias. In addition, claim representatives should work with service providers that are unbiased and have no conflict of interest.

5-3. Claim representatives should be aware of these federal statutes, designed to ensure privacy of confidential information:

a. HIPAA's major goal is to protect individuals' health information while allowing the flow of information to provide and promote high quality healthcare. Claim representatives must be aware of HIPAA restrictions and obtain the necessary authorizations to obtain HIPAA-protected information.

b. Claim representatives must be aware of GLB because it may restrict their access to financial information obtained by their company for a purpose other than a claim, but which would be useful to the claim investigation.

c. The Sarbanes-Oxley Act requires more extensive reporting of claim information, greater accuracy in setting claim reserves, and more extensive audits of claims and claim files.

d. Claim representatives should be aware of the restrictions imposed by the Fair Credit Reporting Act should they find it necessary to obtain or disclose an insured's or a claimant's financial information during a claim investigation. Claim representatives should check with their supervisors or managers to determine what "reasonable procedures" are in place to protect the confidentiality of this information.

5-4. It is important for a claim file to provide a complete and accurate account of all the activities and actions taken by the claim representative because a claim file may be read by many different people, each with a different purpose. Regardless of who reads the file, no reader should be left wondering why something did or did not happen or how a conclusion was reached.

5-5. In addition to their own experience, claim representatives can consult with sources inside and outside the insurance company, including these:

- Co-workers

- Supervisors and managers

- Defense lawyers who are already involved in the case

- Other defense lawyers who are not involved in the case

- People who represent a typical jury

- Computer-generated damage or injury evaluations

- Jury verdict research companies

5-6. Although claim representatives must make realistic offers and carefully consider all demands, lawyers are not held to the same standard. They can make exaggerated demands in a vigorous representation of their clients, and their clients often expect them to do so, in the hope of obtaining the best settlement possible.

5-7. Regular and prompt communication with the insured achieves several important results, including these:

- The insured feels like a part of the defense and can offer assistance.

- The insured can participate in discussions about the possibility of settlement and the handling of the claim.

- The correspondence with the insured documents the insurer's good-faith claim handling and the basis for its judgment about settlement.

- The correspondence establishes that the insured gave the insurer informed consent to take on the defense of the case and to decide how to defend it.

5-8. These are three critical elements of good-faith claim handling:

- Consistent supervision

- Thorough training

- Manageable caseloads

Direct Your Learning

Adjusting Property and Liability Claims

Educational Objectives

After learning the content of this assignment, you should be able to:

1. Explain how and why the activities in the framework for handling property claims are accomplished.

2. Describe the challenges of adjusting the following types of property claims:

   - Residential dwelling claims

   - Residential personal property claims

   - Commercial structure claims

   - Business income claims

   - Merchandise claims

   - Transportation and bailment claims

   - Catastrophe claims

3. Explain how and why the activities in the framework for handling a liability claim are accomplished.

4. Describe the challenges of handling each of the following types of claims:

   - Auto bodily injury liability claims

   - Auto property damage claims

   - Premises liability claims

   - Operations liability claims

   - Products liability claims

   - Workers compensation claims

   - Professional liability claims

Educational Objectives, continued

5. Given a claim, determine coverage for a loss using the framework for coverage analysis and the activities in the claim handling process.

Outline

▶ **Property Claim Handling Process**

A. Who Has an Insurable Interest? Who Is an Insured?
   1. Interests in Property
   2. Policy Requirements for an Insurable Interest
   3. Identification of Insureds
B. What Property Is Insured? Where Is It Insured? When Is It Insured?
   1. Property Type and Location
   2. Policy Period
C. What Are the Covered Causes of Loss?
   1. Direct and Indirect Loss
   2. Physical and Nonphysical Loss to Property
   3. Exclusions and Verification of Causes of Loss
D. What Is the Dollar Amount of Loss?
   1. Replacement Cost
   2. Actual Cash Value
   3. Deductibles
   4. Stated Values and Agreed Amounts
   5. Repair or Replace Option
   6. Appraisal Clause
E. What Are the Insured's Duties After a Loss?
   1. Provide Prompt Notice
   2. Protect Property
   3. Assist With the Loss Adjustment Process
   4. Provide Proof of Loss
   5. Submit to Examination Under Oath
F. What Procedures Are Used to Conclude a Claim?
   1. Determining the Cause of Loss
   2. Determining the Amount of Loss
   3. Documenting the Cause and Amount of Loss
   4. Determining Salvage Value and Subrogation Rights

▶ **Handling Specific Types of Property Claims**

A. Residential Dwelling Claims
   1. Insured's Concerns
   2. Additional Living Expense
   3. Contractors
   4. Restoration and Cleaning Services
B. Residential Personal Property Claims
   1. Inventory
   2. Depreciation
   3. Sublimits
   4. Scheduled Property
C. Commercial Structure Claims
   1. Architects and Contractors
   2. Property's Actual Cash Value
   3. Problems With Mortgageholders
   4. Contamination and Pollution Cleanup
   5. Arson Investigation
D. Business Income Claims
   1. Identifying the Best Loss Settlement Approach
   2. Determining Business Income Loss
   3. Determining the Period of Restoration
   4. Determining Extra Expense Amounts
   5. Consulting Accountants to Determine Amounts
E. Merchandise Claims
   1. Merchandise Valuation
   2. Salvage
   3. Reporting Form Losses
   4. Importance of Negotiation
F. Transportation and Bailment Claims
   1. Insurance Coverages
   2. Legal Liability
G. Catastrophe Claims
   1. Pre-Loss Planning
   2. Post-Loss Planning

▶ **Liability Claim Handling Process**

A. Determining Coverage
   1. Claimant's Allegations
   2. Coverage Problems
   3. Bodily Injury and Property Damage
   4. Intentional Acts
   5. Contractual Obligations
   6. Property Under the Insured's Control

 Repetition helps students learn. Read, write, and repeat key points for each assignment.

B. Determining Legal Liability
1. Investigation
2. Tort Liability
3. Criminal Liability
4. Contractual Liability
5. Statutory Liability
6. Vicarious Liability
7. Defenses to Liability Claims
C. Determining Damages
1. Bodily Injury Claims
2. Property Damage Claims
D. Negotiating and Settling Claims
E. Litigation Process
1. Role of Courts in Resolving Claims
2. Duty to Defend

▶ Handling Specific Types of Liability Claims
A. Auto Bodily Injury Liability Claims
1. Coverage Determination
2. Accident Reconstruction
3. Coordination With Auto No-Fault and Workers Compensation
4. Uninsured Motorists Coverage
5. Underinsured Motorists Coverage
B. Auto Property Damage Claims
1. Constructive Total Losses
2. Agreed Repair Prices
C. Premises Liability Claims
1. Determining the Cause of the Accident
2. Determining Comparative Negligence
D. Operations Liability Claims
1. Bases of Liability
2. Contractual Assumptions of Liability
3. Preservation of the Accident Scene
E. Products Liability Claims
1. Bases of Liability
2. Product and Manufacturer Identification
3. Use of Experts
4. Review of Warnings and Instructions
5. Improper Use
F. Workers Compensation Claims
1. Investigating Compensation Cases
2. Controlling Medical Expenses

3. Controlling Disability Expenses
G. Professional Liability Claims
1. Determining Standard of Care
2. Determining Damages
3. Defending Malpractice Claims

▶ The Framework for Coverage Analysis and the Claim Handling Process Case Study
A. Case Facts
B. Case Analysis Tools
C. Activities in the Claim Handling Process
D. Acknowledging and Assigning the Claim
E. Identifying the Policy and Setting Reserves
F. Contacting the Insured or the Insured's Representative
G. Investigating the Claim
H. Documenting the Claim
I. Determining Cause of Loss, Liability, and Loss Amount
1. Property Damage Claims
2. John's Medical Claim
3. Karen's Medical Claim
J. Concluding the Claim

For each assignment, you should define or describe each of the Key Words and Phrases and answer each of the Review and Application Questions.

Educational Objective 1
Explain how and why the activities in the framework for handling property claims are accomplished.

Key Words and Phrases

Depreciation

Broad evidence rule

Agreed amount

Review Questions

1-1. In a property claim, what is a general way to answer the question "Who has an insurable interest"?

1-2. What questions can claim representatives ask to determine whether fixtures are real property?

1-3. Identify four exclusions that can complicate the answer to the question "What are the covered causes of loss?"

1-4. When claim representatives determine the answer to "What is the dollar amount of the loss?," what issues must they consider?

1-5. In what ways must an insured assist with the property loss adjustment process to meet his or her duties after a loss?

1-6. In the conclusion activity for a property claim, what procedure can help minimize the insurer's loss after the loss payment is made?

Educational Objective 2

Describe the challenges of adjusting the following types of property claims:

- **Residential dwelling claims**
- **Residential personal property claims**
- **Commercial structure claims**
- **Business income claims**
- **Merchandise claims**
- **Transportation and bailment claims**
- **Catastrophe claims**

Key Words and Phrases

Sublimit

Prospective settlements

Retrospective settlements

Business income

Period of restoration

Bill of lading

Released bill of lading

Review Questions

2-1. Describe the claim representative's priorities following a serious loss to a home.

2-2. Explain how the obligation to provide an inventory for residential personal property claims is met by the insured when written records are unavailable.

2-3. Why does an insurer have more flexibility with scheduled property than with ordinary personal property in settling a residential personal property claim?

2-4. Why are the values of commercial structures more difficult to determine than the values of residences?

2-5. Explain how failure to report inventory levels promptly to the insurer can penalize the insured in the event of a merchandise loss.

2-6. Explain how and why a claim representative's claim handling under a carrier/bailee policy differs from that of most property coverage claims.

2-7. Describe the pre- and post-loss activities that can assist insurers when catastrophes occur.

Application Questions

2-8. Bookseller is an independently owned bookstore located in an urban shopping area. A fire makes the property untenantable, causing a suspension in business operations. Explain the special claim considerations facing the claim representative in handling Bookseller's business income loss.

2-9. Ducane Manufacturing is moving its operations and has hired a common carrier to transport several large pieces of equipment to Ducane's new location. While being unloaded from the common carrier's truck, a piece of equipment falls off a forklift and is severely damaged. What factors would a claim representative need to consider to determine whether the common carrier is liable for this damage? Explain.

Educational Objective 3
Explain how and why the activities in the framework for handling a liability claim are accomplished.

Key Words and Phrases

Proximate cause

Hold-harmless agreement (or indemnity agreement)

Assumption of risk

Comparative negligence

Contributory negligence

Pain and suffering

Bad-faith claim

Structured settlement

Advance payment

Walk-away settlement

Review Questions

3-1.   What are the four steps in handling a liability claim?

3-2.   What determines coverage in a liability claim? Explain the reason for this.

3-3. Explain the problems that claim representatives face—when determining liability—related to the intentional act exclusion.

3-4. Why would a claim representative cover topics in a statement with which witnesses are likely to be unfamiliar?

3-5. Explain why it is necessary for a claim representative to understand all of the elements of tort liability.

3-6. Describe the defenses that insurers may use when a claim involves charges of negligence against its insured.

3-7. Explain the difference between special damages and general damages in bodily injury claims.

3-8. Under what circumstances does an insurer have a legal obligation to settle?

3-9. Explain why structured settlements are mutually beneficial for the insurer and the claimant.

3-10. Explain why it is often in the best interests of the claimant and defense lawyers to settle claims without going to court.

Application Question

3-11. Harrison decided to use an insecticide, manufactured by Zappi Enterprises, to exterminate the tent caterpillars that infested his trees in late summer and early fall. While spraying the insecticide, Harrison noticed that the chemical mist carried from his trees onto his grass and the grass of the adjoining neighbor. One of the neighbor's children became ill. The child's father has brought a claim against Zappi.

a. When considering coverage for property under the insured's control, would Zappi's liability insurer be likely to find coverage for this claim?

b. Would Zappi's liability insurer defend Zappi if a lawsuit ensued?

Educational Objective 4

Describe the challenges of handling each of the following types of claims:

- **Auto bodily injury liability claims**
- **Auto property damage claims**
- **Premises liability claims**
- **Operations liability claims**
- **Products liability claims**
- **Workers compensation claims**
- **Professional liability claims**

Key Words and Phrases

Constructive total loss

Warranty

Express warranty

Preferred provider organization (PPO)

Medical management

Review Questions

4-1. What details of an auto accident can an accident reconstruction expert ascertain that a claim representative can use to help determine coverage?

4-2. Under what circumstances would a claim representative determine a damaged auto to be a constructive total loss?

4-3. Describe the standards of care that property owners owe to trespassers, licensees, and business invitees.

4-4.   What two questions should a claim representative ask regarding assumption of liability?

4-5.   What are bases for liability under products coverage?

4-6.   Describe how claim representatives should handle claimants who were injured by products that may have been used improperly.

4-7.   Describe the actions insurers have taken to control the rising costs of workers compensation related medical expenses.

4-8.   Describe the standard of care to which professionals are held.

Application Question

4-9. Refined Insurance Company has been notified that an explosion and fire occurred at a large refinery operated by one of its insureds. The explosion and fire caused extensive injuries to the insured's employees and to visiting sales representatives.

   As a result of this loss, Refined will be faced with the settlement of many kinds of losses, including premises liability and workers compensation. Briefly describe the unique elements or problems associated with the settlement of each of these types of losses.

Educational Objective 5

Given a claim, determine coverage for a loss using the framework for coverage analysis and the activities in the claim handling process.

Application Questions

5-1. Mary owns a 2010 Volkswagen CC and lives in a state that does not have no-fault auto laws. Mary insures her CC with Danford Insurance under a Personal Auto Policy (PAP) with towing coverage and an uninsured motorist (UM) coverage endorsement. Mary returned to her car after shopping to find a large dent in the rear passenger fender and the rear bumper hanging to the ground on one side. A streak of light blue paint on the bumper suggested it had been struck by another vehicle, but there was no other indication of who was responsible for the damage.

   Mary immediately phoned Danford's claim center to report the loss. The telephone representative advised Mary to contact the police and to request a copy of the police report after it has been filed. He also advised Mary that she had towing coverage, which would pay up to $45 to tow her car if the damage is covered by her policy.

   Mary contacted the police department and answered questions for Officer Wills, who arrived at the scene and investigated the incident. Officer Wills gave Mary an accident form to complete and submit to the police department. Then Mary had her car towed to a repair facility.

Danford assigned the claim to its claim representative, Adam, who reviewed Mary's coverage and set a $1,000 UM reserve and a $45 towing reserve in Danford's claim system based on Danford's loss reserve guidelines. Next, Adam phoned Mary to ask for details of the loss. Adam arranged to inspect the damage to Mary's vehicle the following day and asked to meet Mary at the scene of the loss to confirm the location so he could personally investigate. Adam added notes to the electronic claim file to explain his activity to date and created a diary entry to obtain the police report.

Based on these details of the loss, which of the following activities in the claim handling process had Danford or Adam completed? Explain your answers.

5-2. John is a telecommuter who works in his basement office and uses his personal computer to perform his work and correspond with his employer. In addition to John's office, the finished basement includes a recreation room with a sofa, loveseat, several overstuffed chairs, and a pool table. John insures his home under an HO-3 (2000) policy with XYZ Insurance. While John was away from his home for several hours, the hose on his washing machine burst, and water ran over the floor of the first-floor laundry room and absorbed into the carpet in the adjoining hallway, which kept it from flowing further. Water also poured into a floor register and seeped down through the floor into the basement. By the time John returned home and discovered the problem, the entire basement was flooded with foot-deep water.

In addition to the damage to the furnishings and pool table, the central processing unit of John's computer, which sits on the floor in his office, was damaged. The utility room tile and hall carpet on the first floor were water-damaged, along with the basement carpeting, paneling, and ceiling tile. John reported the water damage claim to his insurance agent, who forwarded the information to XYZ. Use the claim handling process, and apply the framework for coverage analysis as a guide to show how a claim representative would handle this claim.

a. The first activity in the claim handling process is acknowledging and assigning the claim. XYZ sent an automatic notification to John's agent to confirm that it received his claim and to inform him that the claim was assigned to Tom, an XYZ claim representative. What other action might Tom take at this stage in the process?

b. What is the next activity in the claim handling process, and how should Tom complete that activity?

c. As part of the framework for coverage analysis on a property claim, what questions should Tom answer as he reviews the policy?

d. Assume that Tom confirmed these facts:

John is the named insured.

A+ Rate Mortgage is listed on the declarations page as a mortgageholder for the home.

Replacement cost coverage for the damage to the structure, including the tile floor, carpets, paneling, and ceiling tile, is provided under Coverage A—Dwelling with a $200,000 limit and a $500 deductible.

Coverage for the furnishings, pool table, and computer is provided under Coverage C—Personal Property with a $100,000 limit and an endorsement that provides replacement cost coverage for personal property.

Coverage C, subpart 4i, Property Not Covered includes business data stored in computers and related equipment. However, the subpart explains that the cost of blank recording or storage media is covered, along with any prerecorded computer programs available in the market.

A special limit of liability of $2,500 applies to the computer under part C3h of the HO-3 for property on the residence premises used primarily for business purposes.

Coverage was in force at the time of the loss.

Section I—Perils Insured Against, part A provides coverage for the dwelling for mold, fungus, or wet rot; however, under part A, subpart 2c(5) excludes coverage for such damage if the mold, fungus, or wet rot is hidden within walls or ceilings, or beneath the floor or above the ceilings, if caused by overflow of water from a household appliance.

Section I—Perils Insured Against, part B, subpart 12 provides coverage for the computer for damage caused by accidental discharge or overflow of water from within a household appliance; however, it does not provide coverage for the damaged washing machine hose.

Section I—Exclusions, part A3 Water damage does not apply to this loss.

What is the next activity in the claim handling process? Assuming John has not retained a lawyer, a public adjuster, or any other representative, how should Tom complete this activity?

e. Assume that Tom will complete the entire investigation and claim handling process. John confirmed that he had bought the washing machine and hose new a year before the loss and that he had not had any previous problems with the machine or hose. What is the next activity in the claim handling process, and what questions should Tom ask as part of this activity?

f. Tom would begin the investigation during his visit with John. What actions would Tom perform to complete the investigation?

g. What ongoing activity in the claim handling process would Tom complete in conjunction with other activities?

h. Assuming John has met all of the insured's duties after a loss, what is the final question Tom should consider in a property claim? What activities in the claim handling process are involved in answering that question?

i. During his visit to John's home, Tom inspected the faulty washing machine and the extent and location of the damage to affirm that the burst washing machine hose was the cause of the loss. He also verified, by the condition of the carpeting and the computer, that the computer was most likely on the floor and damaged when the flooding occurred. What other actions should Tom take to determine the cause of loss, liability, and the loss amount?

j. It was determined that John's two-year-old computer should be replaced. Therefore, John asked about the value of the company data on his hard drive. How should Tom respond to that question?

k. Tom determined that the burst washing machine hose was indeed the cause of the water damage, and he determined the following values based on the estimates and receipts:

Cost of remediation—$2,500

Costs to tear out and replace building materials—$30,100

Costs to replace personal property, excluding the computer—$18,000

Cost to replace the computer with a new model of like kind—$1,000

Cost of inspection and estimates on computer—$80

Cost to rent a temporary replacement computer—$45 for one month

Total loss—$51,725

As part of the claim conclusion, what policy provisions must Tom apply to determine the total loss amount? Explain how he would apply these provisions.

l. What policy provisions must Tom apply to the total loss to determine the amount of the initial payment he could make to John for the loss? Explain how Tom would apply the provision.

m. Depending on XYZ's guidelines, why might Tom issue two separate checks or drafts to John for this loss—one for the damage to the dwelling and one for the damage to the personal property? Indicate what policy provision could dictate this action, and explain why.

n. To comply with state and federal laws, what other checks must Tom perform before he issues any payments to John for this loss?

o. Assuming John had no outstanding legal payment obligations, John was satisfied with the settlement provisions, and no dispute ensued, what other actions must Tom take to conclude the claim?

Answers to Assignment 8 Questions

NOTE: These answers are provided to give students a basic understanding of acceptable types of responses. They often are not the only valid answers and are not intended to provide an exhaustive response to the questions.

Educational Objective 1

1-1. Generally, anyone who would be financially harmed by the destruction of property has an insurable interest in that property.

1-2. Claim representatives can ask these questions to determine whether fixtures are real property:

- How permanently attached is the fixture to the real property?

- Is the fixture well adapted to the real property?

- What was the intent of the owner (when adding the fixture)?

1-3. Four exclusions that can complicate whether the cause of loss is covered are these:

- Gradual causes of loss

- Ordinance or law

- Faulty design, construction, or material

- Intentional acts of the insured

1-4. When determining the dollar amount of the loss, the claim representative must consider whether replacement cost, actual cash value, or stated values or agreed amounts apply and how the appropriate amount is calculated. The claim representative must determine whether a deductible applies to the loss and, if so, how it should be applied. The claim representative must determine whether the insurer should apply repair or replace options. In addition, if the insurer or the insured chooses to invoke the appraisal clause, the claim representative must understand the appraisal process and consider how the appraisal clause influences the value of the loss.

1-5. An insured must inventory all damaged and, under certain policies, all undamaged property; show the damaged property to the claim representative; and provide to the claim representative all books and other records to be inspected. Some policies explicitly require the insured to cooperate.

1-6. When they are applicable to the loss, determining salvage value and subrogation rights and related activities can help minimize the insurer's loss after the loss payment is made.

Educational Objective 2

2-1. The claim representative's priorities are these:

- Assisting the insured in ensuring the physical safety of the insured's family

- Assisting the insured in ensuring the safety and security of the damaged home and its contents to prevent further damage

- Explaining the coverage and the claim handling process to the insured

2-2. In most instances, the claim representative can jog the insured's memory by going through a checklist of types of property. Included in such a checklist might be major furniture in each room, clothes (by category) for each person in the household, drapes, rugs, towels and linens, and so forth.

2-3. Scheduled coverage usually identifies the property precisely. In the event of a claim, the claim representative can contact merchants and appraisers who specialize in such property to determine whether it can be repaired, whether it can be replaced through a secondary market, how much its value has decreased, and whether the insurer can buy replacements at discount.

2-4. For commercial structures, large values are involved, and complex repair and valuation issues exist that require expert assistance.

2-5. Under a reporting-form policy, the insured may be penalized for failing to submit merchandise reports when due as required by the policy. In the event of a loss, the claim representative will not pay more than the amount last reported.

2-6. A claim representative handling claims under a carrier/bailee policy must usually settle two claims arising out of the same property loss: the owner's and the carrier/bailee's. The carrier/bailee has an interest in the property to the extent of its earned fees. Additionally, the carrier/bailee might be legally liable to the owner for the property's return.

2-7. Pre-loss planning: Claim departments should have a sufficient number of claim representatives available in potential disaster areas while maintaining service throughout the rest of the country. Claim offices in disaster-prone areas should have kits prepared that provide all materials that a visiting claim representative may need (forms, maps, telephone directories, clipboards, calculators, etc.). Administrative departments must be prepared to rent office space, have equipment installed and furniture available, and procure temporary living quarters and rental cars on short notice.

Post-loss planning: The circumstances of catastrophes will cause claim representatives to modify normal claim procedures, and claims may be paid with less documentation than usual. Insurers might reimburse the insured's own labor in cleaning up the property. Claims that would normally require an in-person inspection might be handled with phone calls.

2-8. One of the first considerations is whether to settle the loss prospectively or retrospectively. Retrospective settlements, or those taking place after the property has been repaired, are more common. Settlements before the property is repaired, or prospective settlements, are used in cases in which the insured does not intend to make repairs or intends to make significant alterations.

The next consideration is determining the business income loss; a Business Income Report/Work Sheet can help determine this figure. The claim representative must also consider the period of restoration and how soon the policyholder can resume business operations, as well as any extra expenses the insured may have incurred to avoid or minimize the suspension of the business.

2-9. A claim representative handling transportation losses must review the policy providing coverage, because the policy may provide coverage for other parties. Policies for carriers typically protect both the owner of the property and the carrier. In the absence of an agreement to the contrary, common carriers are liable for damage to an owner's goods. The only exceptions are for acts of God, war, negligence of the shipper, exercise of public authority, and inherent vice of the goods.

Educational Objective 3

3-1. The four steps in handling a liability claim are (1) determining coverage, (2) determining legal liability, (3) determining damages, and (4) negotiating and settling the claim.

3-2. The claimant's allegations determine coverage, even if those allegations are disputed and even if they are eventually proved untrue. Liability policies protect the insured against legal claims and the cost to defend them, regardless of whether the claims are valid or groundless.

3-3. Claim representatives cannot rely on the intentional act exclusion unless they are familiar with the law in their state regarding its meaning. For example, in some states, an assault might not be excluded as an intentional act unless the insured intended the resulting harm. This standard makes the exclusion much harder to apply than in states that consider an intentional assault covered as long as the insured intended to commit the assault. States that require an indication that the insured intended the harm do not require that the insured intended the precise harm that occurred. Furthermore, the intent to cause harm might be inferred from the commission of the assault.

3-4. A claim representative should cover these areas to prevent the witness from inventing evidence on these points at a later time.

3-5. A claim representative investigating tort liability must know all of the elements of the tort(s) in question so that tort liability can be recognized.

3-6. Defenses include absence of negligence, comparative or contributory negligence in cases in which a claimant's own fault contributes to causing his or her bodily injury, and assumption of risk in cases in which the claimant knows of a risk and voluntarily assumes it anyway. Statutes of limitations may also serve as a defense. Each state imposes time limits on the right to file lawsuits, and the amount of time varies by state and by type of legal claim.

3-7. Damages can be classified as either special damages or general damages. Special damages are established for losses that can be quantified, such as loss of earnings. General damages are for intangible losses, such as pain and suffering. General damages are highly subjective, but they are the largest and most important element of damages in bodily injury claims.

3-8. Courts require insurers to make reasonable efforts to settle within policy limits and to accept settlement offers within policy limits whenever the value of the claim exceeds policy limits.

3-9. Structured settlements are especially useful when the claimant is likely to experience regular damages into the future, such as loss of income, or when the claim representative suspects that the claimant might be unable to effectively manage a lump-sum payment. They are attractive to insurers because they enable insurers to offer a larger total settlement at a lower present cost than with a lump-sum payment. Structured settlements are often funded through annuities, and the present cost of an annuity is less than what the annuity will pay in the future.

3-10. It is generally in the best interests of the claimant and defense lawyers to settle out of court because of the stress, adverse psychological effects, time constraints, costs, and uncertain outcomes of a trial.

3-11.

    a.   Although property damage to property that the insured has sold or given away is excluded from typical liability policies, claims for consequential bodily injury and damage to another's property are usually covered. Consequently, Zappi's insurer would be likely to find coverage for the claim.

    b.   Yes. Zappi's liability insurer would defend any lawsuit for damages potentially covered under the liability policy, even if the suit were groundless or unprovable.

Educational Objective 4

4-1.   An accident reconstruction expert can help determine the vehicle speed and what a driver should have been able to see at the time of an accident. They can also judge by the skid marks when and where the driver first reacted to a hazard and they can usually establish the exact time of day and the weather conditions at the time of the accident.

4-2.   When the cost to repair a vehicle plus its remaining salvage value equals or exceeds the vehicle's pre-loss value, the vehicle is a constructive total loss. However, should the insured want to keep the auto, the claim representative is entitled to pay the claim based on the actual cash value.

4-3.   An owner owes only slight care to a trespasser and cannot intentionally inflict injury. For licensees, who are on the premises for their own benefit, the owner owes an intermediate duty. Business invitees, who are on the premises for the benefit of the owner, are owed a high duty of care.

4-4.   A claim representative examining an assumption of liability clause must determine whether it requires defense and indemnity or just indemnity. Questions that help affirm this are: "Does the assumption of liability extend to all liabilities of the indemnified party or just to liabilities that arise out of the indemnifying party's behavior?" and "Does the assumption of liability extend to the owner of the project site or to the indemnified party's subcontractors?"

4-5.   Other than the traditional negligence theories, products liability may be based on breach of warranty or strict liability in tort.

4-6.   Claim representatives who suspect improper use should obtain detailed statements from the claimants. If the claimant is not available for a statement, the claim representative might be able to obtain an account of what happened from the claimant's emergency-room records or from an initial report by the claimant to a state or federal consumer products regulatory agency.

4-7.   Insurers have taken many steps to manage rising workers compensation medical costs, including making arrangements with preferred provider organizations (PPOs) through which the insurer receives a discount on the usual medical expenses in exchange for a volume of referrals. Insurers also conduct medical bill audits to identify charges that are excessive, fabricated, or redundant. Utilization review services control medical expenses by determining whether medical treatment is necessary. Medical management controls medical expenses on claims that involve high medical costs, such as permanent bodily injuries.

4-8.   Professionals are required to exercise the standard of care accepted in their profession.

4-9.   These are the unique elements and problems associated with each of these types of losses:

- Premises liability—Injury to the visiting sales representatives should be investigated as premises liability claims. Claim representatives who handle premises liability claims must establish good rapport with the claimant, both to establish the cause of the accident and to determine comparative negligence.

  Typically, the claimant asserts that the insured failed to maintain the premises in a reasonably safe condition. The standard of care for property owners is traditionally qualified by the claimant's status on the premises. A property owner owes a high level of care to business invitees. Almost any factor in the environment of the insured premises contributing to the accident could indicate negligence on the insured's part. When investigating premises liability claims, claim representatives should solicit statements from the claimant and all witnesses who can testify about either the accident or the condition of the accident scene. If the scene is substantially the same as when the accident occurred, the claim representative should take photographs.

- Workers compensation—Work-related injuries are compensated without regard to fault and generally without the involvement of lawsuits. Claim representatives handling these types of claims must investigate the cases thoroughly. This investigation will involve medical expenses and time lost from work. The claim representative will need to review not only medical records but also documentation regarding earnings.

Educational Objective 5

5-1.   These activities have been completed as specified:

- Acknowledge and assign the claim—Danford assigned the claim to Adam, who acknowledged the claim in his phone call to Mary.

- Identify the policy and set reserves—Adam identified Mary's policy by reviewing the policy information and setting UM and towing reserves.

- Contacting the insured or the insured's representatives—Adam contacted the insured via his phone call to Mary. He also arranged to meet her the next day at the loss scene.

- Investigating the claim—Adam began the claim investigation by reviewing the policy for Mary's available coverages, but much of the investigation is still pending.

- Documenting the claim—Adam began documentation of the claim by recording notes on the claim activities and by setting a diary entry to get a police report.

5-2. By using the facts of the case, using the claim handling process, and applying the framework for coverage analysis, these answers are one possibility to address the questions regarding the case study:

    a. Tom might enter the basic claim information from the loss notice into XYZ's claim computer system, if that was not already completed, and he would call John for details on the cause of the loss and the extent of damage. Tom would probably recommend that John contact a restoration company to mitigate the loss by pumping out the water and using drying techniques to help avoid mold. Tom would set up a time within the next few days to inspect the loss, and he would instruct John to retain the damaged personal property until the claim was concluded. Additionally, Tom would discuss any concerns John has about the claim, including the need for a damage estimate on the computer and any temporary measures needed to replace the computer.

    b. The next activity is identifying the policy and setting reserves. While Tom may have done an initial review of the policy before contacting John, he would now perform a more in-depth review, using the framework for coverage analysis, to determine what types of coverage apply to the loss. Also, Tom must set some minimal reserves for the claim according to XYZ's internal reserving guidelines and based on his conversation with John—such as $5,000 for the dwelling and $5,000 for the personal property. If any coverage concerns are apparent, Tom should notify John through a nonwaiver agreement or a reservation of rights letter to protect XYZ's interests while continuing the claim investigation.

    c. Tom should answer the following questions in this review:

        • Who has an insurable interest, and who is an insured?

        • What property is insured? Where is it insured? When is it insured?

        • What are the covered causes of loss?

    d. The next activity in the claim handling process is contacting the insured or the insured's representative. Because Tom has already set up an appointment with John, to prepare for his meeting Tom should compile a list of questions to ask John and could prepare a set of instructions for John, explaining how the claim will be handled and what actions John should complete.

       Tom should contact John and visit John's home so he can inspect the damage and discuss the facts of the loss (or assign the inspection to another claim representative, if such a visit is impractical). If he hasn't already, Tom should explain the inspection, appraisal, and investigation process and explain any portions of the investigation that he will perform.

       Tom should ask John whether the washing machine has ever been repaired and whether the hose has ever been replaced.

       Tom should write the estimate for repair or replacement of the structure. He should give John a Proof of Loss form, including a personal property inventory, to complete and return.

       Tom should ask John to obtain an estimate for repair or replacement of the computer with an assessment that would confirm that water was the cause of the damage. Finally, Tom should explain the approximate time needed to settle the loss. Tom might also ask John for any receipts for the original purchases of his computer and other personal property.

e.   The next activity in the process is investigating the claim. Questions that Tom should ask include these:

•   What is the dollar amount of loss?

•   What are the insured's duties after a loss?

f.   Tom should prepare an estimate for removal and replacement of the tile flooring, carpet, paneling, and ceiling tile. Tom should also ask John for any receipts from the loss mitigation firm and for any receipts related to temporarily replacing the computer. Once John has obtained a repair or replacement estimate for the computer, Tom should ask for that estimate and any receipt from a technician who completed the estimate. Additionally, Tom should review the Conditions in the HO-3 to ensure that John has met all of the insured's duties after a loss in Section I—Conditions, part B.

g.   Tom would document all information on the claim in his file status notes and would collect other claim documentation such as the receipts, the Proof of Loss statement/inventory, the damage estimates, and any other written documents for inclusion in the claim file. Tom might use a diary system to note crucial dates in the process, and he may need to complete internal and external reports according to XYZ's claim policies. At this time, Tom should also adjust the loss reserves to more accurately reflect the dollar amounts from his estimates, from the inventory John prepared, and from the computer estimate John provided.

h.   The final question Tom should consider is, "What procedures are used to conclude the claim?" Answering this question involves the last two activities in the claim handling process:

•   Determining the cause of loss, liability, and the loss amount

•   Concluding the claim

i.   Tom should make diagrams of the damaged areas and take photos of the damage to the structure, furnishings, pool table, and computer and any other evidence that supports (or negates) the loss description. He should review the repair/replace estimate on the computer to verify that water was the likely cause of damage to the computer. He should follow XYZ's procedures for verifying the values of the personal property, for comparison with John's inventory and with the estimate for repair or replacement of the computer. Doing so may include checking a personal property database for like kind replacement of the property and printing the documentation for inclusion in the claim file. If the computer could be repaired, Tom should determine from the information collected whether XYZ should pay for the repair or replacement of the computer. Liability is not an issue in this first-party property claim because there was no evidence that any technician had serviced the washing machine or the hose, which could have contributed to the hose's bursting. Tom should verify that he has all of the receipts and estimates, and then he should calculate the loss amounts accordingly.

j.   Tom should explain that the unendorsed HO-3 provides no coverage for loss of data from a covered loss, as described in Coverage C4, Property Not Covered, subpart i. He should explain that XYZ would only pay for the replacement of the blank media—in this case, the disk drive—and would not be likely to pay the costs for a professional to transfer the data from the old hard disk drive to the new hard disk drive.

k. Tom must apply the policy limits and sublimits, and the deductible. He must ensure that the loss amounts for the dwelling and for the personal property are at or below the policy limits and that the computer loss amount is at or below the sublimit for business equipment. The $32,600 total dwelling and remediation loss is less than the $200,000 dwelling limit. The total for the personal property loss, including the computer and its associated expenses, is $19,125, which is less than the $100,000 personal property limit. And the $1,000 computer loss is less than the $2,500 sublimit. Tom would then subtract the $500 deductible from the total ($51,725 – $500) to get $51,225.

l. John's HO-3 provides replacement cost coverage for his dwelling, and an endorsement provides replacement cost coverage for his personal property. To determine the initial loss payment, Tom would calculate the loss to the structure and to the personal property based on their actual cash value (ACV—subject to depreciation). Tom would deduct the difference between the ACV and the replacement cost from the total loss payment. He would explain to John that once all the building materials have been replaced or repaired and as he replaces his personal property with like kind property, he can submit his receipts and obtain the additional amounts allowed for replacement cost.

m. Because A+Rate Mortgage has an insurable interest in the dwelling and is listed as a mortgageholder in the declarations, XYZ's guidelines may require that Tom make the check/draft for the dwelling payable to both John and A+Rate Mortgage. Tom would make the check/draft for the personal property payable only to John because no lienholder exists for the property.

n. Tom must check all state and federal databases, as required, to ensure that no other party is entitled to any claim payment that John would otherwise receive. Such interests could be created by tax or child support obligations, for example.

o. Because of the extent of the water damage, it is unlikely that any salvage recovery could be obtained.

Tom would issue checks/drafts for the designated payments to John and would follow up with supplemental payments when he receives the final receipts for John's dwelling repairs and replacements and personal property replacements. Most insurers would not list the mortgageholder on the final check/draft for the dwelling, because it would be restored to value at that point. Tom might also request that John sign and return a settlement agreement.

Tom would complete his documentation of the claim by ensuring that all receipts, photos, diagrams, forms, signed settlement agreement, and other documentation are included in the file; by completing his file status notes to explain the steps taken to resolve the claim; and by describing the final resolution and settlement decisions. At that time, he would also close any open claim reserves.

Tom might set a diary entry when initially making the claim payment to follow up with John on submitting his final receipts for repair or replacement of the building materials and personal property, according to XYZ's guidelines for such reimbursement, and he would remove the diary entry after he had received all the receipts.

Tom would also complete any required internal and external reports for this claim according to XYZ's guidelines, including any closing report when all actions on the claim have been completed.

Direct Your Learning

Actuarial Operations

Educational Objectives

After learning the content of this assignment, you should be able to:

1. Describe the actuarial function in insurer operations and the actuarial services required by insurers.

2. Describe the insurer goals of ratemaking and the ideal characteristics of rates.

3. Describe the components of an insurance rate and common ratemaking terms.

4. Explain how the following factors can affect ratemaking:

   - Estimation of losses

   - Delays in data collection and use

   - Change in the cost of claims

   - Insurer's projected expenses

   - Target level of profit and contingencies

5. Describe the following ratemaking methods:

   - Pure premium

   - Loss ratio

   - Judgment

6. Describe each of the following steps in the ratemaking process:

   - Collect data

   - Adjust data

   - Calculate the indicated overall rate change

   - Determine territorial and class relativities

   - Prepare and submit rate filings to regulatory authorities as required.

Educational Objectives, continued

7. Describe the policy-year, calendar-year, accident-year, and report-year data aggregation methods.

8. Explain how the following ratemaking factors vary by type of insurance:

    - Experience period

    - Trending

    - Large loss limitations

    - Credibility

    - Increased limits factors

9. Describe the purpose and types of loss reserves, the importance of accurate estimation of loss reserves, and techniques used by actuaries in their analysis.

Outline

▶ **The Actuarial Function**
  A. What is an Actuary?
  B. Actuarial Functions
  C. Actuarial Services

▶ **Insurer Ratemaking Goals**
  A. Ratemaking Goals
  B. Ideal Characteristics of Rates
    1. Stable
    2. Responsive
    3. Provide for Contingencies
    4. Promote Risk Control
    5. Reflect Differences in Risk Exposure

▶ **Rate Components and Ratemaking Terms**
  A. Rate Components
  B. Ratemaking Terms
  C. Investment Income

▶ **Factors That Affect Ratemaking**
  A. Estimation of Losses
  B. Delays in Data Collection and Use
  C. Change in Cost of Claims
  D. Insurer's Projected Expenses
  E. Target Level of Profit and Contingencies

▶ **Ratemaking Methods**
  A. Pure Premium Ratemaking Method
    1. Fixed and Variable Expenses
  B. Loss Ratio Ratemaking Method
  C. Judgment Ratemaking Method

▶ **Ratemaking Process Overview**
  A. Collect Data
  B. Adjust Data
    1. Adjust Premiums to Current Rate Level
    2. Adjust Historic Experience for Future Development
    3. Apply Trending to Losses and Premium
  C. Calculate Indicated Overall Rate Change
  D. Determine Territorial and Class Relativities
  E. Prepare and Submit Rate Filings

▶ **Ratemaking Data Aggregation Methods**
  A. Policy-Year Method
  B. Calendar-Year Method
  C. Accident-Year Method
  D. Report-Year Method
  E. Illustration

▶ **Ratemaking Factor Variances for Different Types of Insurance**
  A. Experience Period
  B. Trending
  C. Large Loss Limitations
  D. Credibility
  E. Increased Limits Factors

▶ **Loss Reserves and Analysis**
  A. Purpose of Loss Reserves
  B. Types of Loss Reserves
  C. Importance of Accurate Loss Reserves
  D. Analysis of Loss Reserves
  E. Loss Development—a Closer Look

Find complete information regarding exam dates and fees at www.TheInstitutes.org/forms. Plan to register with The Institutes well in advance of your exam. If you have any questions, or need updated registration information, contact The Institutes.

For each assignment, you should define or describe each of the Key Words and Phrases and answer each of the Review and Application Questions.

Educational Objective 1
Describe the actuarial function in insurer operations and the actuarial services required by insurers.

Key Word or Phrase

Data mining

Review Questions

1-1. Describe the areas covered in the actuarial examination process, other than mathematical models and statistical techniques.

1-2. Explain why an insurer with staff actuaries might also retain actuarial consultants.

1-3. Describe the tasks performed by actuaries at advisory organizations.

Educational Objective 2
Describe the insurer goals of ratemaking and the ideal characteristics of rates.

Key Word or Phrase

Ratemaking

Review Questions

2-1. Describe the primary goal of ratemaking.

2-2. Name the three rate characteristics on which regulation is generally based.

2-3. List the five characteristics that rates should have to enable an insurer to be competitive and make a reasonable profit.

Educational Objective 3
Describe the components of an insurance rate and common ratemaking terms.

Key Words and Phrases
Rate

Premium

Pure premium

Expense provision

Underwriting expenses

Loss adjustment expense (LAE)

Allocated loss adjustment expenses (ALAE)

Unallocated loss adjustment expenses (ULAE)

Underwriting profit

Review Questions

3-1. Describe the three components of an insurance rate.

3-2. List the six basic ratemaking terms.

3-3. Explain why an insurer's loss reserves for liability insurance are usually much greater than its loss reserves for an equivalent amount of property insurance.

Educational Objective 4

Explain how the following factors can affect ratemaking:

- **Estimation of losses**
- **Delays in data collection and use**
- **Change in the cost of claims**
- **Insurer's projected expenses**
- **Target level of profit and contingencies**

Key Words and Phrases

Ultimate loss

Experience period

Investment income

Review Questions

4-1. Why are accurate loss reserve estimates important?

4-2. What factors cause a lag in reflecting loss experience in ratemaking?

4-3. Describe factors that can affect the frequency and severity of claims.

Application Question

4-4. Danforth Insurance Co. has an auto insurance portfolio consisting of 100,000 insured vehicles in a territory. Danforth analyzes the losses for this portfolio during a three-year period.

a. If the amount of incurred losses is $30 million during the three-year period, what pure premium rate should Danforth use?

b. Assume that the reserves in the incurred losses are inadequate by $3 million. What should the pure premium rate be?

c. If Danforth used the rate based on $30 million in losses, what would Danforth's loss be the following year, assuming that the $33 million in incurred losses was correct?

Educational Objective 5

Describe the following ratemaking methods:

- **Pure premium**
- **Loss ratio**
- **Judgment**

Key Words and Phrases

Pure premium method

Loss ratio method

Judgment ratemaking method

Review Questions

5-1. Describe the pure premium ratemaking method.

5-2. What are the components of the expense provision in the pure premium method?

5-3. Identify the two loss ratios used in the loss ratio ratemaking method.

5-4. Determine the effect on rates if the actual loss ratio is less than the expected loss ratio when the loss ratio ratemaking method is used.

5-5. List the types of insurance that use judgment rates to determine premiums.

Educational Objective 6

Describe each of the following steps in the ratemaking process:

- **Collect data**
- **Adjust data**
- **Calculate the indicated overall rate change**
- **Determine territorial and class relativities**
- **Prepare and submit rate filings to regulatory authorities as required.**

Key Words and Phrases

Loss cost multiplier

Calendar-year method

Policy-year method

Accident-year method

On-level factor

Loss development factor

Exponential trending

Review Questions

6-1. Describe the three general categories of data that insurers collect for ratemaking.

6-2. Explain why data must be adjusted after it is collected for ratemaking, and describe the methods actuaries use to adjust premium and loss data for ratemaking.

6-3. Describe territorial relativities and explain how they can be determined.

Educational Objective 7
Describe the policy-year, calendar-year, accident-year, and report-year data aggregation methods.

Key Words and Phrases

Written premiums

Unearned premiums

Bulk reserves

Schedule P

Claims-made coverage

Review Questions

7-1. Identify four ratemaking data aggregation methods.

7-2. What are the two major disadvantages associated with the policy-year ratemaking data collection method?

7-3. Describe the calendar-year method.

7-4. Under the calendar-year method, how are earned premiums calculated?

7-5. Contrast the report-year method with the accident-year method.

7-6. Why does the accident-year method eliminate the largest source of error inherent in the calendar-year method?

Educational Objective 8
Explain how the following ratemaking factors vary by type of insurance:

- **Experience period**
- **Trending**
- **Large loss limitations**
- **Credibility**
- **Increased limits factors**

Key Words and Phrases

Basic limit

Catastrophe model

Credibility

Credibility factor

Increased limit factor

Risk charge

Review Questions

8-1. Identify the three factors that should be considered in determining an appropriate experience period.

8-2. Describe the special trending problem that exists in workers compensation insurance.

8-3. Explain how the effects of large losses are controlled in ratemaking calculations?

8-4. Explain why increased limits factors frequently exceed 100 percent of the charge for basic coverage limits in liability insurance.

Educational Objective 9

Describe the purpose and types of loss reserves, the importance of accurate estimation of loss reserves, and techniques used by actuaries in their analysis.

Key Words and Phrases

Incurred but not reported (IBNR) reserves

Actuary

Review Questions

9-1. Identify the two principal types of loss reserves.

9-2. Describe the three components of bulk reserves.

9-3. Explain how inaccurate reserves can affect an insurer's financial condition.

9-4. Contrast the expected loss ratio method of estimating losses with the loss development method of estimating losses.

Answers to Assignment 9 Questions

NOTE: These answers are provided to give students a basic understanding of acceptable types of responses. They often are not the only valid answers and are not intended to provide an exhaustive response to the questions.

Educational Objective 1

1-1. In addition to mathematical models and statistical techniques, the actuarial examination process covers insurance operations, accounting, insurance law, and financial analysis.

1-2. Outside actuaries can supplement staff knowledge with specialized expertise, provide independent opinion when needed, and ease workload peaks. Regulatory authorities and reinsurers sometimes require insurers to provide a consulting actuary's opinion verifying the accuracy and reasonableness of the staff actuaries' work.

1-3. Actuaries at advisory organizations collect premium and loss data from many insurers to use in calculating expected loss costs for various types of insurance and maintain contact with regulatory authorities to facilitate approval of rate filings.

Educational Objective 2

2-1. The primary goal of ratemaking is to develop a rate structure that enables the insurer to compete effectively while earning a reasonable profit on its operations. To accomplish this, the rates must result in premiums that adequately cover all losses and expenses and that leave a reasonable amount for profits and contingencies.

2-2. Rate regulation is generally based on having rates that are adequate, not excessive, and not unfairly discriminatory.

2-3. Rates should be stable, be responsive, provide for contingencies, promote loss control, and reflect differences in risk exposure.

Educational Objective 3

3-1. The three components of an insurance rate are these:

    a. An amount needed to pay future claims and loss adjustment expenses

    b. An amount needed to pay future expenses

    c. An amount for profit and contingencies

3-2. The six basic ratemaking terms are exposure base, earned exposure unit, pure premium, expense provision, loss adjustment expenses, and profit and contingencies.

3-3. An insurer's loss reserves for liability insurance are usually higher than those for property insurance because property losses are usually paid relatively quickly, while liability losses often are not paid until years after losses occur.

Educational Objective 4

4-1. Rates are calculated based on loss reserve estimates. If the estimates are too low, the calculated rates will be too low, and insufficient funds will be available to pay for losses sustained by the insurer. If the estimates are too high, rates will be too high.

4-2. The principal sources of a lag in reflecting loss experience in ratemaking are delays by policyholders in reporting losses to insurers, the time required to analyze data and complete rate filings, delays in obtaining approval from regulators, the time required to implement new rates, and the time period during which rates are in effect.

4-3. Economic deflation or inflation can affect the cost (severity) of claims. Legislative and regulatory changes can affect the number (frequency) of claims.

4-4.

    a. There are 300,000 car-years insured (100,000 cars per year × 3 years).

       $30,000,000 (losses) ÷ 300,000 (car years) = $100

       A premium rate of $100 per year will cover losses, according to the previous experience.

    b. $33,000,000 (losses) ÷ 300,000 (car years) = $110

       A premium rate of $110 per year will cover losses, according to the experience.

    c. Danforth charged a premium rate of $100 per car per year for 100,000 cars.

       This resulted in premium of $10 million.

       However, if Danforth had used a premium rate of $110, this would have resulted in premium of $11 million. Thus, the loss to Danforth is $1 million.

Educational Objective 5

5-1. The pure premium method involves calculating the pure premium, or the amount needed to pay losses and, in some cases, allocated loss adjustment expenses. Expenses per exposure unit are then estimated, and then the profit and contingencies factor is determined. Finally, the pure premium is added to the expense provision and divided by one minus the profit and contingencies factor.

5-2. The expense provision can be separated into two components: fixed expenses and variable expenses. Fixed expenses are stated as a dollar amount; variable expenses are stated as a percentage of the rate.

5-3. The loss ratio method uses two loss ratios—the actual loss ratio and the expected loss ratio of the insurer during the selected experience period.

5-4. If the actual loss ratio is less than the expected loss ratio, a rate reduction is indicated.

5-5. The judgment method is used for some types of insurance, such as ocean marine insurance, some inland marine classes, aviation insurance, and situations when limited data are available, as with terrorism coverage.

Educational Objective 6

6-1. Insurers collect data regarding losses, both paid and incurred; earned premium and/or exposure information; and expenses, including a profit and contingencies factor.

6-2. Data must be adjusted because the raw exposure, premium, and loss data reflect conditions from present and past periods, whereas the rates being developed will be used in the future.

If rates charged in the experience period were written at different rate levels, actuaries adjust premiums to the current level. Actuaries also adjust historic loss experience for future development, usually by applying loss development factors. Another method is to apply trending to losses and premium by projecting historic environmental changes into the future.

6-3. Territorial relativities reflect the extent to which various subsets of insureds in a state deserve rates that are higher or lower than the statewide average rate.

Territorial relativities can be determined by comparing the estimated loss ratio (or pure premium) for each geographic territory to the statewide average loss ratio (or pure premium). This comparison produces factors that are applied to the statewide average rate to reflect experience in each geographic territory.

Educational Objective 7

7-1. These are four ratemaking data aggregation methods:

- Policy-year method
- Calendar-year method
- Accident-year method
- Report-year method

7-2. Two major disadvantages apply to the policy-year ratemaking data collection method:

- It takes longer to gather data for this method than for the other methods.
- There is additional expense to gather data by policy year.

7-3. The calendar-year method involves aggregating data from accounting records to estimate earned premiums and incurred losses.

7-4. Under the calendar-year method, earned premiums are calculated using this formula:

Earned premiums = Written premiums for the year + (Unearned premiums at the beginning of the year – Unearned premiums at the end of the year)

7-5. The report-year method is similar to the accident-year method, except that claims are aggregated by when the claim was reported rather than when it occurred. Premiums used in this method are the same calendar-period earned premiums used with the accident year method.

7-6. The accident-year method eliminates the largest source of error inherent in the calendar-year method because accident-year losses arise only from insured events that occur during the period and therefore are not affected by changes in reserves for events that occurred in other periods.

Educational Objective 8

8-1.   These are the three factors that should be considered in determining an appropriate experience period:

- Any legal requirements

- The variability of losses over time

- The credibility of the resulting ratemaking data

8-2.   Because the benefits for such insurance are established by statute, legislation or a court decision can change the benefits unexpectedly.

8-3.   In liability insurance, the effects of large losses are controlled by using only basic limit losses in calculating incurred losses. Workers compensation has no basic limits, so individual claims are limited to a specified amount for ratemaking purposes. For property insurance, only part of a large single loss is included in the ratemaking calculations in the state in which the loss occurred. The balance is then spread over the rates of all the states. Most losses from catastrophic events are excluded from ratemaking data and replaced by a flat catastrophe charge in the rates.

8-4.   Increased limits factors frequently exceed 100 percent of the charge for basic coverage limits for these reasons:

- Additional coverage purchased by the customer can be much higher than the basic limit.

- Although loss severity does not increase uniformly with increased coverage limits, the exposure to loss is substantially greater at higher limits.

- Higher limits can also require a portion of the coverage to be reinsured, with the additional expense of reinsurance included in the rate.

- Because large losses occur less frequently than small losses and take longer to settle, the variability of losses in higher coverage layers is greater than for the basic limit losses, and the credibility is lower. This greater variability requires a greater risk charge at higher levels of coverage.

Educational Objective 9

9-1.   The two principal types of loss reserves established by insurers are case reserves and bulk reserves.

9-2.   Bulk reserves have these three components:

- Incurred but not reported (IBNR) reserves

- Reserves for losses that have been reported but for which the established case reserves are inadequate

- Reserves for claims that have been settled and then reopened

9-3.   Loss reserves (including loss adjustment expenses reserves) often exceed the total surplus for an insurer and are usually a considerable multiple of the earnings in a year. A significant change in reserves for prior years not only affects the current year's profitability but also can risk the insurer's solvency.

9-4. The expected loss ratio method uses a prior estimate of ultimate losses rather than current experience. The loss development method assumes that future changes in the loss will occur in a similar manner as in the past. This latter method assumes that the experience to date is an indicator of what future payments will be.

Direct Your Learning

Reinsurance

Educational Objectives

After learning the content of this assignment, you should be able to:

1. Describe reinsurance and its principal functions.

2. Describe the three sources of reinsurance.

3. Describe treaty reinsurance and facultative reinsurance.

4. Describe the types of pro rata reinsurance and excess of loss reinsurance and their uses.

5. Describe finite risk reinsurance and other methods that rely on capital markets as alternatives to traditional and non-traditional reinsurance.

6. Describe the factors that should be considered in the design of a reinsurance program.

7. Given a case, identify the reinsurance needs of an insurer and recommend an appropriate reinsurance program to address those needs.

8. Explain how reinsurance is regulated.

Outline

▶ **Reinsurance and Its Functions**

    A. Basic Terms and Concepts

    B. Reinsurance Functions

        1. Increase Large-Line Capacity

        2. Provide Catastrophe Protection

        3. Stabilize Loss Experience

        4. Provide Surplus Relief

        5. Facilitate Withdrawal From a Market Segment

        6. Provide Underwriting Guidance

▶ **Reinsurance Sources**

    A. Professional Reinsurers

    B. Reinsurance Departments of Primary Insurers

    C. Reinsurance Pools, Syndicates, and Associations

    D. Reinsurance Professional and Trade Associations

        1. Intermediaries and Reinsurance Underwriters Association (IRU)

        2. Brokers & Reinsurance Markets Association (BRMA)

        3. Reinsurance Association of America (RAA)

▶ **Reinsurance Transactions**

    A. Treaty Reinsurance

    B. Facultative Reinsurance

▶ **Types of Reinsurance**

    A. Pro Rata Reinsurance

        1. Quota Share Reinsurance

        2. Surplus Share Reinsurance

    B. Excess of Loss Reinsurance

        1. Per Risk Excess of Loss

        2. Catastrophe Excess of Loss

        3. Per Policy Excess of Loss

        4. Per Occurrence Excess of Loss

        5. Aggregate Excess of Loss

▶ **Alternatives to Traditional Reinsurance**

    A. Finite Risk Reinsurance

    B. Capital Market Alternatives to Traditional and Non-Traditional Reinsurance

▶ **Reinsurance Program Design**

    A. Factors Affecting Reinsurance Needs

        1. Growth Plans

        2. Types of Insurance Sold

        3. Geographic Spread of Loss Exposures

        4. Insurer Size

        5. Insurer Structure

        6. Insurer Financial Strength

        7. Senior Management's Risk Tolerance

    B. Factors Affecting Retention Selection

        1. Maximum Amount the Primary Insurer Can Retain

        2. Maximum Amount the Primary Insurer Wants to Retain

        3. Minimum Retention Sought by the Reinsurer

        4. Co-participation Provision

    C. Factors Affecting Reinsurance Limit Selection

        1. Maximum Policy Limit

        2. Extra-Contractual Obligations

        3. Loss Adjustment Expenses

        4. Clash Cover

        5. Catastrophe Exposure

▶ **Reinsurance Program Design Case Studies**

    A. Atley Insurance Company

        1. Situation 1

        2. Situation 2

    B. Medical Malpractice Insurance Company

▶ **Reinsurance Regulation**

    A. Contract Certainty

    B. Credit for Reinsurance Transactions

If you find your attention drifting, take a short break to regain your focus.

For each assignment, you should define or describe each of the Key Words and Phrases and answer each of the Review and Application Questions.

Educational Objective 1
Describe reinsurance and its principal functions.

Key Words and Phrases

Reinsurance

Primary insurer

Reinsurer

Reinsurance agreement

Insurance risk

Retention

Reinsurance premium

Ceding commission

Retrocession

Retrocedent

Retrocessionaire

Large-line capacity

Line

Surplus relief

Portfolio reinsurance

Novation

Review Questions

1-1. Briefly define reinsurance.

1-2. What is the purpose of a retrocession?

1-3. What are some of the practical business goals that reinsurance can help an insurer achieve?

1-4. What are the six principal functions that reinsurance performs for primary insurers?

1-5. How does increasing its large-line capacity allow an insurer to grow?

1-6. What are three ways in which a primary insurer can use reinsurance to stabilize its loss experience?

1-7. How may a primary insurer completely eliminate the liabilities it has assumed under the policies it has issued?

Educational Objective 2
Describe the three sources of reinsurance.

Key Words and Phrases

Professional reinsurer

Direct writing reinsurer

Reinsurance intermediary

▶▶

Reinsurance pools, syndicates, and associations

Reinsurance pool

Syndicate

Association

Review Questions

2-1. Identify the three sources from which reinsurance may be purchased.

2-2. Describe the role of a reinsurance intermediary.

2-3. What factors should a primary insurer evaluate when considering a reinsurer?

2-4. Describe the function of reinsurance pools, syndicates, and associations.

2-5. List three of the most widely known reinsurance professional and trade associations.

Educational Objective 3
Describe treaty reinsurance and facultative reinsurance.

Key Words and Phrases

Adverse selection

Facultative certificate of reinsurance

Review Questions

3-1. Contrast treaty reinsurance and facultative reinsurance.

3-2. Explain why primary insurers usually make treaty reinsurance agreements so their underwriters do not have to exercise discretion in using reinsurance.

3-3. Identify the four functions of facultative reinsurance.

Educational Objective 4
Describe the types of pro rata reinsurance and excess of loss reinsurance and their uses.

Key Words and Phrases

Pro rata reinsurance

Flat commission

Profit-sharing commission

Sliding scale commission

Quota share reinsurance

Catastrophe excess of loss reinsurance

Surplus share reinsurance

Bordereau

Line guide

Excess of loss reinsurance (nonproportional reinsurance)

Attachment point

Subject premium

Working cover

Co-participation provision

Per risk excess of loss reinsurance

Loss occurrence clause

Per policy excess of loss reinsurance

Per occurrence excess reinsurance

Clash cover

Extracontractual damages

Excess of policy limits loss

Aggregate excess of loss reinsurance

Review Questions

4-1. Identify the two basic types of reinsurance transactions.

4-2. What are the two principal approaches that reinsurers use to allocate losses?

4-3. What is the distinguishing characteristic of quota share reinsurance?

4-4. Explain how the amount of insurance, the premium, and losses are allocated under a pro rata reinsurance agreement.

4-5. What is the distinguishing characteristic of surplus share reinsurance?

4-6. Under what circumstance will a reinsurer respond to a loss under an excess of loss reinsurance agreement?

4-7. What are the two most common approaches to handling loss adjustment expenses under an excess of loss reinsurance agreement?

4-8. Describe the application of per risk excess of loss reinsurance.

4-9. Describe how a loss occurrence clause functions within a catastrophe excess of loss reinsurance agreement.

4-10. Describe the purpose of catastrophe excess of loss reinsurance.

4-11. Explain how per policy excess of loss reinsurance functions.

4-12. Explain how per occurrence excess of loss reinsurance functions.

4-13. For what types of liability insurance is clash cover useful?

4-14. What type of losses does aggregate excess of loss reinsurance cover?

Educational Objective 5

Describe finite risk reinsurance and other methods that rely on capital markets as alternatives to traditional and non-traditional reinsurance.

Key Words and Phrases

Finite risk reinsurance

Capital market

Securitization of risk

Special purpose vehicle (SPV)

Insurance derivative

Contingent capital arrangement

Insurance-linked security

Surplus note

Strike price

Review Questions

5-1. Describe the type of losses that finite risk reinsurance generally is designed to cover.

5-2. Explain why a finite risk reinsurance agreement typically has a multi-year term.

5-3. List and briefly describe some of the more commonly used capital market alternatives to reinsurance.

Educational Objective 6
Describe the factors that should be considered in the design of a reinsurance program.

Key Words and Phrases

Reinsurance program

Underwriting risk

Review Questions

6-1. List the factors primary insurers consider to determine their reinsurance needs.

6-2. Identify three reasons why a primary insurer expecting rapid premium growth is likely to need additional reinsurance.

6-3. Contrast the reinsurance needs of primary insurers selling personal insurance with those selling commercial insurance.

6-4. What effect may a wide geographic spread of loss exposures have on an insurer's reinsurance needs?

6-5.   Contrast the reinsurance needs of small primary insurers with those of large primary insurers.

6-6.   Why does an insurer that is financially strong need less reinsurance than a financially weaker one?

6-7.   What senior management characteristic is most significant to its reinsurance decision making?

6-8.   Identify the four factors, in addition to cost, that affect a primary insurer's retention selection.

6-9. What two factors determine the maximum amount that a primary insurer can retain?

6-10. Describe the purpose of a minimum retention requirement.

6-11. Identify the five factors related to the selection of reinsurance treaty limits.

Educational Objective 7
Given a case, identify the reinsurance needs of an insurer and recommend an appropriate reinsurance program to address those needs.

Application Questions

7-1. Over the last several years, Greenly Insurance Company has rapidly expanded the number of properties it insures in hurricane-prone areas. It is concerned that its reinsurance program may be inadequate for its growing catastrophe exposure. How may it amend its reinsurance program to address this concern?

7-2. Tarton Insurance Company has emerged as the leading commercial property insurer in an area where industrial growth has exploded throughout the decade as companies seeking to cut costs have relocated to exploit the region's favorable tax treatment. Although Tarton's program for insuring office condominiums has thus far supported the growth in its business, it believes that continued expansion in the region could create commercial property insurance demands that it may be unable to satisfy. Ideally, Tarton would like to be equipped to write accounts that need high property coverage limits while continuing to grow its business. How could Tarton and its reinsurers configure a reinsurance program to achieve these objectives?

7-3. Liability Insurer is concerned that a disproportionate number of its insureds are located in states where an overly litigious environment has led to numerous successful lawsuits against insureds. How could a reconfigured reinsurance program address this concern?

Educational Objective 8
Explain how reinsurance is regulated.

Key Words and Phrases

Insolvency clause

Intermediary clause

Review Questions

8-1. Describe the regulatory requirements to which reinsurers must adhere.

8-2. Describe the relationship between reinsurance rates and primary insurer rates.

8-3. What is the general requirement associated with the concept of contract certainty?

8-4. Why are primary insurers usually eager to take credit against their unearned premiums and loss reserves for premiums paid to and losses recoverable from reinsurers?

8-5. Describe the function of an insolvency clause.

Answers to Assignment 10 Questions

NOTE: These answers are provided to give students a basic understanding of acceptable types of responses. They often are not the only valid answers and are not intended to provide an exhaustive response to the questions.

Educational Objective 1

1-1. Reinsurance is the transfer from one insurer to another of some or all of the financial consequences of certain loss exposures covered by the primary insurer's policies.

1-2. Under a retrocession, one reinsurer, the retrocedent, transfers all or part of the reinsurance risk that it has assumed or will assume to another reinsurer, the retrocessionaire.

1-3. Reinsurance helps an insurer achieve several practical business goals, such as insuring large exposures, protecting policyholders' surplus from adverse loss experience, and financing the insurer's growth.

1-4. Although several of its uses overlap, reinsurance is a valuable tool that can perform six principal functions for primary insurers:

   • Increase large-line capacity

   • Provide catastrophe protection

   • Stabilize loss experience

   • Provide surplus relief

   • Facilitate withdrawal from a market segment

   • Provide underwriting guidance

1-5. Increasing large-line capacity allows a primary insurer to assume more significant risks than its financial condition and regulations would otherwise permit.

1-6. A primary insurer can stabilize loss experience by obtaining reinsurance to accomplish any, or all, of these purposes:

   • Limit its liability for a single loss exposure

   • Limit its liability for several loss exposures affected by a common event

   • Limit its liability for loss exposures that aggregate claims over time

1-7. A primary insurer can completely eliminate the liabilities it has assumed under the insurance policies it has issued through a novation. A novation is not considered portfolio reinsurance because the substitute insurer assumes the direct obligations to insureds covered by the underlying insurance.

Educational Objective 2

2-1.   Reinsurance can be purchased from three sources:

- Professional reinsurers

- Reinsurance departments of primary insurers

- Reinsurance pools, syndicates, and associations

2-2.   Reinsurance intermediaries generally represent a primary insurer and work with that insurer to develop a reinsurance program that is then placed with a reinsurer or reinsurers.

2-3.   The primary insurer should evaluate the reinsurer's claim-paying ability, reputation, and management competence before entering into the reinsurance agreement.

2-4.   Reinsurance pools, syndicates, and associations provide member companies the opportunity to participate in a line of insurance with a limited amount of capital—and a proportionate share of the administrative costs—without having to employ the specialists needed for such a venture.

2-5.   Three of the most widely known reinsurance professional and trade associations are these:

- Intermediaries and Reinsurance Underwriters Association (IRU)

- Brokers & Reinsurance Markets Association (BRMA)

- Reinsurance Association of America (RAA)

Educational Objective 3

3-1.   In treaty reinsurance, the reinsurer agrees in advance to reinsure all the loss exposures that fall within the treaty. Although some treaties allow the reinsurer limited discretion in reinsuring individual loss exposures, most treaties require that all loss exposures within the treaty's terms must be reinsured.

In facultative reinsurance, the primary insurer negotiates a separate reinsurance agreement for each loss exposure that it wants to reinsure. The primary insurer is not obligated to purchase reinsurance, and the reinsurer is not obligated to reinsure loss exposures submitted to it.

3-2.   Primary insurers usually make treaty reinsurance agreements so their underwriters do not have to exercise discretion in using reinsurance. If treaty reinsurance agreements permitted primary insurers to choose which loss exposures they ceded to the reinsurer, the reinsurer would be exposed to adverse selection.

3-3. Facultative reinsurance serves these four functions:

- Facultative reinsurance can provide large line capacity for loss exposures that exceed the limits of treaty reinsurance agreements.

- Facultative reinsurance can reduce the primary insurer's exposure in a given geographic area.

- Facultative reinsurance can insure a loss exposure with atypical hazard characteristics and thereby maintain the favorable loss experience of the primary insurer's treaty reinsurance and any associated profit-sharing arrangements.

- Facultative reinsurance can insure particular classes of loss exposures that are excluded under treaty reinsurance.

Educational Objective 4

4-1. The two types of reinsurance transactions are treaty reinsurance and facultative reinsurance.

4-2. The principal approaches that reinsurers use to allocate losses are broadly defined as pro rata reinsurance and excess of loss reinsurance.

4-3. The distinguishing characteristic of quota share reinsurance is that the primary insurer and the reinsurer use a fixed percentage in sharing the amounts of insurance, policy premiums, and losses (including loss adjustment expenses).

4-4. Under a pro rata reinsurance agreement, the amount of insurance, the premium, and the losses (including loss adjustment expenses) are divided between the primary insurer and the reinsurer in the same proportions as the risk.

4-5. The distinguishing characteristic of surplus share reinsurance is that when an underlying policy's total amount of insurance exceeds a stipulated dollar amount, or line, the reinsurer assumes the surplus share of the amount of insurance (the difference between the primary insurer's line and the total amount of insurance).

4-6. In an excess of loss reinsurance agreement, also called "non-proportional reinsurance," the reinsurer responds to a loss only when the loss exceeds the primary insurer's retention, often referred to as the attachment point.

4-7. These are the two most common approaches to handling loss adjustment expenses:

- Prorate the loss adjustment expenses between the primary insurer and the reinsurer based on the same percentage share that each is responsible for the loss.

- Add the loss adjustment expenses to the amount of the loss when applying the attachment point of the excess of loss reinsurance agreement.

4-8. Per risk excess of loss reinsurance applies separately to *each loss* occurring to *each risk*, with the primary insurer usually determining what constitutes one risk (loss exposure).

4-9. A loss occurrence clause specifies a time period, in hours, during which the primary insurer's losses from the same catastrophic occurrence can be aggregated and applied to the attachment point and reinsurance limits of the catastrophe excess of loss reinsurance agreement. Such clauses usually specify a time period of 72 consecutive hours (3 days) for hurricane losses and 168 consecutive hours (7 days) for earthquake losses.

4-10. Catastrophe excess of loss reinsurance protects the primary insurer from an accumulation of retained losses that arise from a single catastrophic event.

4-11. Per policy excess of loss reinsurance is used primarily with liability insurance. It applies the attachment point and the reinsurance limit separately to each insurance policy issued by the primary insurer, regardless of the number of losses occurring under each policy.

4-12. Per occurrence excess of loss reinsurance applies the attachment point and the reinsurance limit to the total losses arising from a single event affecting one or more of the primary insurer's policies.

4-13. Clash cover may be useful for types of liability insurance in which loss adjustment expenses are likely to be very high and the underlying per occurrence reinsurance limits include these expenses rather than pro rate them.

4-14. Aggregate excess of loss reinsurance can be used for property or liability insurance and covers aggregated losses that exceed the attachment point and occur over a stated period, usually one year.

Educational Objective 5

5-1. Generally, finite risk reinsurance is designed to cover high-severity losses.

5-2. A finite risk reinsurance agreement typically has a multi-year term (for example, three to five years) to allow the risk and losses to be spread over several years, while being subject to an aggregate limit for the agreement's entire term.

5-3. Some of the more commonly used capital market alternatives to reinsurance include these:

- Catastrophe bond—a type of insurance-linked security that is specifically designed to transfer insurable catastrophe risk to investors

- Catastrophe risk exchange—a means through which a primary insurer can exchange a portion of its insurance risk for another insurer's

- Contingent surplus note—a surplus note that has been designed so a primary insurer, at its option, can immediately obtain funds by issuing notes at a pre-agreed rate of interest

- Industry loss warranty—an insurance-linked security that covers the primary insurer in the event that the industry-wide loss from a particular catastrophic event, such as an earthquake or hurricane, exceeds a predetermined threshold

- Catastrophe option—an agreement that gives the primary insurer the right to a cash payment from investors if a specified index of catastrophe losses reaches a specified level (the strike price)

- Line of credit—an arrangement in which a bank or another financial institution agrees to provide a loan to a primary insurer in the event the primary insurer suffers a loss

- Sidecar—a limited-existence special purpose vehicle, often formed as an independent company, that provides a primary insurer additional capacity to write property catastrophe business or other short-tail lines through a quota share agreement with private investors

Educational Objective 6

6-1. Primary insurers consider several factors to determine their reinsurance needs, all of which interact to increase or decrease a primary insurer's need for reinsurance:

- Growth plans
- Types of insurance sold
- Geographic spread of loss exposures
- Insurer size
- Insurer structure
- Insurer financial strength
- Senior management's risk tolerance

6-2. A primary insurer that expects rapid premium growth is likely to need more reinsurance for these three reasons:

- Rapid growth can cause a drain on a primary insurer's policyholders' surplus. Pro rata reinsurance provides a replenishment of the primary insurer's policyholders' surplus because of the ceding commission paid by the reinsurer to the primary insurer.

- The loss ratio for a primary insurer's new business is likely to be less stable than the loss ratio for its established business, which has undergone renewal underwriting. Reinsurance, while not abrogating the total loss amount, limits the amount of this loss to the primary insurer's retention amount.

- Reinsurance enables primary insurers to provide larger amounts of coverage than they otherwise would be able to provide.

6-3. Generally, primary insurers selling personal insurance need less reinsurance than those selling commercial insurance because personal insurance loss exposures need relatively lower coverage limits. Additionally, personal insurance loss exposures are more homogeneous and subject to fewer severe hazards than commercial insurance loss exposures. Because of the homogeneity among personal insurance loss exposures, the loss experience is usually more stable than that of commercial insurance loss exposures and therefore more predictable.

6-4. A wide geographic spread may stabilize the insurer's loss ratio and minimize reinsurance needs, especially in property insurance.

6-5. Typically, small primary insurers need proportionately more reinsurance to stabilize loss ratios than large primary insurers. The loss ratio of a large primary insurer is likely to be more stable than the loss ratio of a small one even if the mix of business sold is identical.

6-6. An insurer that is financially strong needs less reinsurance than a financially weaker one for two reasons. First, it does not need surplus relief to increase its premium capacity. Second, it needs less reinsurance to stabilize its loss ratio.

6-7. Although reinsurance decision making may be supported by statistical data and financial models, it usually reflects the senior management's risk tolerance, which is its willingness to assume risk.

6-8.   In addition to cost, four factors are considered when selecting a retention:

- Maximum amount the primary insurer can retain

- Maximum amount the primary insurer wants to retain

- Minimum retention sought by the reinsurer

- Co-participation provision

6-9.   The maximum amount that a primary insurer can retain is a function of regulatory requirements and the primary insurer's financial strength.

6-10. The purpose of a minimum retention requirement is to encourage the primary insurer to implement sound risk control, underwriting, and loss adjustment practices.

6-11. There are five factors to consider in selecting reinsurance treaty limits, which vary depending on the kind of treaty involved:

- Maximum policy limit

- Extra-contractual obligations

- Loss adjustment expenses

- Clash cover

- Catastrophe exposure

Educational Objective 7

7-1.   Greenly may amend its reinsurance program by adding a catastrophe excess of loss reinsurance agreement, which would cover the aggregation of property losses to Greenly that arise from hurricanes and other catastrophic events.

7-2.   Tarton and its reinsurers could develop a reinsurance program that provides both large-line capacity and financing to aid future growth. Such a program could include a surplus share reinsurance treaty, which would allow Tarton and its reinsurers to share coverage limits, premiums, and losses on policies that exceed Tarton's retention. This would help support Tarton's ability to write accounts that need high property coverage limits. It may also include facultative reinsurance, which would provide large-line capacity for risks that exceed the limits of the reinsurance treaties.

7-3.   Liability Insurer's reinsurance program could be reconfigured to include per occurrence excess of loss reinsurance to limit the effect of any one claim. The reinsurance program could also address the possibility that more than one insured could be sued as the result of a single occurrence and that extra-contractual damages or excess policy limits judgments could be awarded by including a clash cover.

Educational Objective 8

8-1.   Reinsurers are required to file financial statements with state regulatory authorities and to adhere to state insurance regulations regarding reserves, investments, and minimum capital and surplus requirements. They must also undergo periodic examination by the appropriate state authorities.

8-2. The regulation of primary insurer rates could indirectly affect reinsurance rates to the extent that reinsurers receive a reinsurance premium based on the premiums of primary insurers. Thus, regulating the primary insurer's rates might place an effective ceiling on the amount the primary insurer can pay for reinsurance.

8-3. Contract certainty generally requires the complete and final agreement of all terms between the insured and insurer by the time the contract is entered into, with contract documentation provided promptly thereafter.

8-4. Primary insurers are usually eager to take credit against their unearned premiums and loss reserves for premiums paid to and losses recoverable from reinsurers because the availability of those credits, referred to as credit for reinsurance, reduces the drain on the primary insurer's surplus from writing new business.

8-5. The insolvency clause, which is required for the primary insurer to take credit for the reinsurance transaction, provides that the primary insurer's insolvency does not affect the reinsurer's liability for losses under the reinsurance agreement.

Direct Your Learning

Insurer Strategic Management

Educational Objectives

After learning the content of this assignment, you should be able to:

1. Describe the strategic management process.

2. Explain how the Five Forces and SWOT methods can be used to analyze the environment in which an insurer operates.

3. Explain how strategies are developed at the corporate, business, functional, and operational levels.

4. Describe the strategic reasons, considerations, and approaches for insurers to expand their operations globally.

5. Given information about an insurer's business strategies, conduct a SWOT analysis of its strategy.

Outline

▶ **Strategic Management Process**

  A. Strategy Formulation

    1. Mission and Vision Statements

    2. Strategy Formulation Steps

  B. Strategy Implementation

  C. Strategy Evaluation

▶ **The Five Forces and SWOT Methods of Analyzing the Environment**

  A. The Five Forces Model

    1. Threat of New Entrants

    2. Threat of Substitute Products or Services

    3. Bargaining Powers of Buyers

    4. Bargaining Power of Suppliers

    5. Rivalry Among Existing Firms

  B. SWOT Analysis

    1. Strengths and Weaknesses

    2. Opportunities and Threats

▶ **Determining Strategy at Different Organizational Levels**

  A. Corporate-Level Strategy

    1. Concentration on a Single Business

    2. Vertical Integration

    3. Diversification

    4. Decline Mode Strategies

  B. Business-Level Strategy

    1. Cost Leadership

    2. Differentiation

    3. Focus

  C. Functional-Level Strategy

  D. Operational-Level Strategy

▶ **Insurers' Global Expansion**

  A. Trends in Global Expansion

  B. Strategic Reasons for Global Expansion

    1. Revenue Growth and Financial Stability

    2. Global Competitiveness

  C. Global Market Considerations

    1. Market Analysis

    2. Economic Considerations

    3. Political Risks

  D. Approaches to Global Expansion

▶ **Strategic Management Case Study**

  A. Case Facts

    1. Greenly Insurance Company—Internal and External Environment

    2. Greenly Insurance Company—Goals

    3. Greenly Insurance Company—Business Strategies

    4. Issues That Prompted the Evaluation

  B. Case Analysis Tools and Information

  C. Case Analysis Steps

    1. Conduct a Current SWOT Analysis

    2. Determine Business Strategies to Be Evaluated

    3. Evaluate Relevant Business Strategies

Before starting a new assignment, briefly review the Educational Objectives of those preceding it.

For each assignment, you should define or describe each of the Key Words and Phrases and answer each of the Review and Application Questions.

Educational Objective 1
Describe the strategic management process.

Key Words and Phrases

Strategic management process

Mission statement

SWOT analysis

Functional structure

Multidivisional structure

Cost leadership

Review Questions

1-1. Identify the three interdependent stages of the strategic management process.

1-2. What elements do insurer mission statements often include?

1-3. Identify the three basic components of strategy formulation.

1-4. What is the first consideration of strategy implementation?

1-5. Identify the four steps of the strategic control process.

Educational Objective 2

Explain how the Five Forces and SWOT methods can be used to analyze the environment in which an insurer operates.

Key Words and Phrases

Five Forces Model

Trend analysis

Review Questions

2-1. Describe the factors in the general environment that managers should consider as part of an environmental assessment.

2-2. List the five forces that drive competition within an industry.

2-3.   How can management use the Five Forces Model as part of an analysis of its task environment?

2-4.   What areas within the company would managers examine to identify organizational strengths?

Educational Objective 3

Explain how strategies are developed at the corporate, business, functional, and operational levels.

Key Words and Phrases

Vertical integration strategy

Related diversification strategy

Unrelated diversification strategy

Harvest strategy

Turnaround strategy

Divestiture strategy

Differentiation strategy

Focused cost leadership strategy

Focused differentiation strategy

Review Questions

3-1. Describe the levels at which strategy is formulated within an organization.

3-2. Compare forward and backward integration in a vertical integration strategy.

3-3. Explain how an insurer could successfully follow a cost leadership approach at the business level.

Application Question

3-4. The XYZ Insurance Company is facing several internal and external challenges in its business operation. Because of a competitive employment market, the insurer has struggled to maintain staffing levels and is having difficulty staffing its headquarters location. In addition to the headquarters location, XYZ has three regional offices throughout the Midwest and Northeast. Because of heavy competition in the types of insurance it writes, XYZ has lost considerable market share in most of its territories and has experienced steadily decreasing profits. What strategies would XYZ's management team evaluate as corporate-level strategy for the company?

Educational Objective 4
Describe the strategic reasons, considerations, and approaches for insurers to expand their operations globally.

Key Words and Phrases
Strategic alliance

Joint venture

Merger

Subsidiary

Review Questions

4-1. Describe the three key strategic reasons why insurers pursue global expansion.

4-2. Describe the three key areas for an insurer to evaluate in making a strategic decision about expansion into a global market.

4-3. Compare the approaches of strategic alliance, merger, and a wholly owned subsidiary for an insurer planning to expand into a global market

Educational Objective 5

Given information about an insurer's business strategies, conduct a SWOT analysis of its strategy.

Key Word or Phrase

Retention ratio

Application Question

5-1. XYZ Insurance Company is a personal lines insurer with headquarters in Chicago and regional offices throughout the Midwest and Northeast. XYZ's reputation as a strong, reliable organization has engendered loyalty among its employees, many of whom have worked for the company for ten years or more. However, because of heavy competition in the types of insurance it writes, XYZ has lost considerable market share in most of its territories and has experienced steadily decreasing profits. XYZ believes that it is losing market share because it has not kept pace with the needs of its existing customers or the buying preferences of prospective customers. Additionally, its research indicates that locally based insurers in each of the regions in which it operates are better equipped to serve insureds because their agents more effectively interact with the local community. Despite these conditions, XYZ believes that it is positioned to rebound, provided it deploys its resources more efficiently. A recent investment in technology has led to development of a Web site that will allow XYZ to provide quotes and accept applications online. It hopes to use the Web site's interactive features to more effectively ascertain its customers' needs and to test the potential appeal of new endeavors such as "green" insurance options, which it currently doesn't offer.

   a.   Identify one of XYZ Insurance Company's strengths.

b.   Identify one of XYZ's weaknesses.

c.   Identify one of XYZ's opportunities.

Answers to Assignment 11 Questions

NOTE: These answers are provided to give students a basic understanding of acceptable types of responses. They often are not the only valid answers and are not intended to provide an exhaustive response to the questions.

Educational Objective 1

1-1. The strategic management process involves three interdependent stages:

- Strategy formulation—creating a plan

- Strategy implementation—putting the plan into action

- Strategy evaluation—monitoring the results to determine whether the plan works as envisioned

1-2. For insurers, mission statements frequently mention financial strength, customer service, and integrity.

1-3. Strategy formulation has these basic components:

- Analysis of external and internal environments

- Development of long-term strategies and organizational goals

- Determination of strategy at different organizational levels

1-4. The first consideration and a crucial component of strategy implementation is designing the structure of the organization.

1-5. The control process has four steps:

- Establish standards

- Create and apply measurements

- Compare actual results to standards

- Evaluate and implement corrective actions if goals are not met

Educational Objective 2

2-1. General environmental factors include demographics, sociocultural, legal, technological, economic, and global factors.

2-2. These are the five forces:

- Threat of new entrants

- Threat of substitute products or services

- Bargaining power of buyers

- Bargaining power of suppliers

- Rivalry among existing firms

2-3. Managers can use the model to evaluate how these forces affect their organization in an effort to better understand their company's position in the industry. This increased understanding will allow management to construct strategies that will assist in building a competitive advantage for their firm.

2-4. Some of the areas that could be examined include managerial expertise, available product lines, the skill levels and competencies of the staff, current strategies, customer loyalty, growth levels, organizational structure, and distribution channels.

Educational Objective 3

3-1. The corporate-level strategy represents the highest strategy level for a diversified organization, and it determines the types of businesses and potential profitability for the organization. Business-level strategy is implemented by an operation or a strategic business unit to support the corporate-level strategy, to be competitive, and to respond to changes in the external environment. Functional-level strategy is carried out by an organization's departments, such as marketing or underwriting. Operational-level strategy is implemented in a department's day-to-day business activities.

3-2. When a company is pursuing a vertical integration strategy, it either produces its own inputs or disposes of its own outputs. Backward integration occurs when an organization produces inputs for processing. Forward integration occurs when an organization sells its product directly to the customer.

3-3. For a company to be successful with a cost leadership business-level strategy, it must seek to achieve cost efficiencies in all aspects of the operation in order to charge a lower price. To successfully pursue this strategy, most products or services must be fairly standardized. An insurer could achieve lower costs through standardizing underwriting guidelines and using technology to automate processes and improve interaction among departments.

3-4. XYZ is struggling and currently operates in a decline mode. Alternatives available to corporate management include following a harvest strategy to gain short-term profits while phasing out a particular product line or exiting the market. If management determined that the company should be reorganized in an effort to return to profitability, it would follow a turnaround strategy. If, however, management decided the best approach were to sell off a portion of its business, it would follow a divestiture strategy. State regulators in each jurisdiction would, of course, affect the decision that managers would make, and the alternatives available to an insurance operation would differ from some of those available to a non-insurance operation.

Educational Objective 4

4-1. These are the three key strategic reasons why insurers pursue global expansion.

    a. Revenue growth is the primary reason that insurers look to global expansion. There are few new potential customers in mature insurance markets, such as the United States. Global markets, especially those in emerging economies, offer growth opportunities.

    b. Insurers expand globally to increase financial stability. Spreading risks worldwide helps to counter the effects of economic downturn in a particular country. Even in a worldwide recession, the potential for growth in emerging markets can offset loss of income from declines in premiums and investment returns. Spreading risk over a diverse base also minimizes the impact of heavy losses in any one segment of the operation.

c. Insurers also expand globally to increase their competitiveness. Global expansion may help in achieving economies of scale and efficiencies that allow an insurer to compete more effectively in both domestic and global markets. A global expansion strategy also provides additional technology and strategic resources. Additionally, a global strategy may allow an insurer to remain competitive in a specific specialty market, such as mining or oil exploration risks.

4-2. These are the three key areas for an insurer to evaluate in making a strategic decision about expansion into a global market.

a. A market analysis of the insurance market in the country the insurer plans to enter is the first key area to evaluate. Factors in the market analysis include financial requirements, potential returns versus capital to be committed, ease of entry, difficulty of withdrawal, competition, distribution channels, and cultural and language differences.

b. Another key area for evaluation is the host country's economic environment. Important considerations include the level of economic stability, monetary policies, the prevailing attitude toward foreign investors, the potential for exchange-rate volatility, the country's gross domestic product, regulation, economic growth, taxation, and personal income levels.

c. Political risk is also an important area to evaluate. Risks include the potential for confiscation of business assets, nationalization of business, laws regarding nonadmitted insurance, terrorism, government changes, kidnap and ransom, civil unrest, and war.

4-3. Strategic alliances have the advantages of bringing together separate areas of expertise and gaining a host-country participant, who can access local markets and who is familiar with local laws, regulations, and customers. The advantage to merger is the ability to combine resources and reduce overhead expenses. A merger may be more efficient than a strategic alliance, but it also may be complicated by the regulations and antitrust laws of more than one country. Acquisition of, or formation of, a wholly owned subsidiary allows for direct ownership and control of assets. However, this approach requires more capital and presents the highest degree of business, political, and economic risk.

Educational Objective 5

5-1. These answers are based on the XYZ Insurance Company case.

a. Any of these elements may be identified as one of XYZ Insurance Company's strengths:

- Because it has regional offices in two areas of the country, XYZ's operations are geographically diverse.

- XYZ has a reputation as a strong, reliable organization, which could benefit it in numerous ways.

- XYZ has an experienced, loyal workforce.

b. Any of these elements may be identified as one of XYZ's weaknesses:

- XYZ's competitors' agents are interacting more effectively with the local community than XYZ's agents are.

- XYZ is unable to keep pace with the needs of existing customers or the buying preferences of prospective customers.

c. Any of these elements may be identified as one of XYZ's opportunities:

- XYZ's resources and reputation will allow it to invest in and promote a Web site that surpasses those of its competitors.

- XYZ's investment in technology will allow it to provide quotes and accept applications online.

- XYZ can use its research and resources to test and develop new endeavors, such as "green" insurance options.

Exam Information

About Institutes Exams

Exam questions are based on the Educational Objectives stated in the course guide and textbook. The exam is designed to measure whether you have met those Educational Objectives. The exam does not test every Educational Objective. Instead, it tests over a balanced sample of Educational Objectives.

How to Prepare for Institutes Exams

What can you do to prepare for an Institutes exam? Students who pass Institute exams do the following:

▶ Use the assigned study materials. Focus your study on the Educational Objectives presented at the beginning of each course guide assignment. Thoroughly read the textbook and any other assigned materials, and then complete the course guide exercises. Choose a study method that best suits your needs; for example, participate in a traditional class, online class, or informal study group; or study on your own. Use The Institutes' SMART Study Aids (if available) for practice and review. If this course has an associated SMART Online Practice Exams product, you will find an access code on the inside back cover of this course guide. This access code allows you to print (in PDF format) a full practice exam and to take additional online practice exams that will simulate an actual credentialing exam.

▶ Become familiar with the types of test questions asked on the exam. The practice exam in this course guide or in the SMART Online Practice Exams product will help you understand the different types of questions you will encounter on the exam.

▶ Maximize your test-taking time. Successful students use the sample exam in the course guide or in the SMART Online Practice Exams product to practice pacing themselves. Learning how to manage your time during the exam ensures that you will complete all of the test questions in the time allotted.

Types of Exam Questions

The exam for this course consists of objective questions of several types.

The Correct-Answer Type

In this type of question, the question stem is followed by four responses, one of which is absolutely correct. Select the *correct* answer.

> Which one of the following persons evaluates requests for insurance to determine which applicants are accepted and which are rejected?
>
> a.   The premium auditor
>
> b.   The loss control representative
>
> c.   The underwriter
>
> d.   The risk manager

The Best-Answer Type

In this type of question, the question stem is followed by four responses, only one of which is best, given the statement made or facts provided in the stem. Select the *best* answer.

> Several people within an insurer might be involved in determining whether an applicant for insurance is accepted. Which one of the following positions is primarily responsible for determining whether an applicant for insurance is accepted?
>
> a.   The loss control representative
>
> b.   The customer service representative
>
> c.   The underwriter
>
> d.   The premium auditor

The Incomplete-Statement or Sentence-Completion Type

In this type of question, the last part of the question stem consists of a portion of a statement rather than a direct question. Select the phrase that *correctly* or *best* completes the sentence.

> Residual market plans designed for individuals who are unable to obtain insurance on their personal property in the voluntary market are called
>
> a.   VIN plans.
>
> b.   Self-insured retention plans.
>
> c.   Premium discount plans.
>
> d.   FAIR plans.

"All of the Above" Type

In this type of question, only one of the first three answers could be correct, or all three might be correct, in which case the best answer would be "All of the above." Read all the answers and select the *best* answer.

> When a large commercial insured's policy is up for renewal, who is likely to provide input to the renewal decision process?
>
> a.   The underwriter
>
> b.   The loss control representative
>
> c.   The producer
>
> d.   All of the above

"All of the following, EXCEPT:" Type

In this type of question, responses include three correct answers and one answer that is incorrect or is clearly the least correct. Select the *incorrect* or *least correct* answer.

> All of the following adjust insurance claims, EXCEPT:
>
> a.   Insurer claim representatives
>
> b.   Premium auditors
>
> c.   Producers
>
> d.   Independent adjusters